The Management of
Information from
Archives

To the memory of
Margaret Hainsworth

Converte, domine, captivitatem nostram, sicut torrens in austro. Qui seminant in lacrimis, in exsultatione metent.

The Management of Information from Archives

Michael Cook

Gower

Published by

Gower Publishing Company Limited,
Gower House,
Croft Road,
Aldershot,
Hants GU11 3HR,
England

Gower Publishing Company,
Old Post Road,
Brookfield,
Vermont 05036,
U.S.A.

British Library Cataloguing in Publication Data
Cook, Michael, 1931–
   The management of information from archives.
   1. Archives
   I. Title
   025.17'14   CD950

   ISBN 0-566-03504-9

Library of Congress Cataloging in Publication Data
Cook, Michael, 1931–
   The management of information from archives.
   Bibliography: P.   includes index.
   1. Archives——administration. 2. Cataloging of archival material. 3. Archives——data processing. 4. Information storage and retrieval systems——archival material.
   I. Title. CD971 .C66 1985 025.17'14 85-22042

   ISBN 0-566-03504-9

Printed in Great Britain by Blackmore Press, Shaftesbury, Dorset.

Contents

Preface

It now seems to be acceptable for books on archives administration to be radical in intention. A few years ago one had at least to avoid the appearance of wishing for significant change. This book seeks to advocate some important new features in the management of archives, and may be the means of importing some of these features into the training of information professionals of all branches.

It is important to point out some of the subjects which are not dealt with in this study. The most pressing of these is conservation, a subject which ought to occupy the attention of society more than it does. The view of this book is, broadly, that conservation is not necessarily central to archives: one can manage and use the information carried by archival media in the same way as one can do this with books and documents; that is, without considering the long-term preservation of the media. Nevertheless, the ultimate survival of the best as part of the common heritage remains an underlying need of society, and therefore should not be despised. Similarly, the equipping and provisioning of an archives service is not dealt with. The present purpose is to describe in outline the nature of the management aims and systems involved in work with archive materials.

By the time this book is available for readers, the first edition of the *Manual of Archival Description* will have appeared. The present author had much to do with the writing of this manual, and the intention is that the two books should be read and used in close conjunction. They complement each other: the manual giving specific recommendations and models on the writing of archival descriptions, and this book containing the background discussion, the general principles, and a push towards viewing archives work as a branch of information management.

There are very many people who deserve thanks for their help, either general or specific, in these linked projects. Since they cannot all be mentioned, I would like to record particular thanks to these colleagues: Hazel Bennett, Clinton Black, Derek Charman, Ron Chesterman, Daphne Douglas, Janet Dudley, Frank Evans, Andy Evborokhai, Kristina Grant,

Jill Hampson, Bruce Jackson, Peter Jones, Alfred Knight-bridge, Richard Light, Len MacDonald, Brian Redwood, Michael Roper, Alan Seaman, Joan Smith, Richard Storey, Hugh Taylor, John Walford, Margi Whittick and Arnott Wilson; other acknowledgements are made in the manual.

I would like to thank the following authors and institutions for allowing the reproduction of items from their materials: the Archival Description Project (University of Liverpool), Berkshire Record Office, British Antarctic Survey, British Library Department of Manuscripts, British Steel Corporation, Cheshire Record Office, Ron Chesterman, East Sussex Record Office, the Modern Records Centre (University of Warwick), Museum Documentation Association, S.C. Newton, the Public Record Office, St John's College (Cambridge), the Society of Archivists, Tyne & Wear Archives Service, West Sussex Record Office.

My wife has been very supportive during the whole project, and Pat Starkey has helped me with the text, as she has with the *Manual of Archival Description*. Bob Hunt drew the figures. I would like to give them all a special mention.

Michael Cook

Abbreviations

AA	*The American Archivist*
AACR2	Anglo-American Cataloguing Rules, 2nd edition
ADPA	*Automatic Data Processing in Archives*
BAS	British Antarctic Survey
BNB	British National Bibliography
BRA	British Records Association
CCF	Common Communications Format
DP	Data processing
ESRO	East Sussex Record Office
FOI	Freedom of information
GUA	Glasgow University Archives
HMC	Royal Commission on Historical Manuscripts
HMT	Historical manuscripts tradition
ICA	International Council on Archives
ISBD	International Standard Bibliographical Description
JSA	*Journal of the Society of Archivists*
LISA	*Library and Information Science Abstracts*
MAD	*Manual of Archival Description*
MDA	Museum Documentation Association
MLWP	Methods of Listing working party
NARS	National Archives and Records Service (USA)
NATIS	National Information System
NBM	Non-book materials
NRA	National Register of Archives
PAT	Public archives tradition
PRO	Public Record Office
RAMP	Records & Archives Management Programme (of UNESCO)
RLIN	Research Libraries Information Network
RM	Records management
SAA	Society of American Archivists
SDI	Selective dissemination of information
SRG	Specialist Repositories Group
UBL	*UNESCO Bulletin for Libraries*
UJISLAA	*UNESCO Journal of Information Science, Librarianship and Archives Administration*

1 Archival management in an information context

This book describes the management of information derived from archival media. There are already several books on archives administration, and rather fewer on records management. In both fields, the literature has taken its starting point from the existing practice of an archives or records management service. In most cases this was one of the large national archives services: the British Public Record Office in the case of Sir Hilary Jenkinson,[1] the American National Archives and Records Service in the case of T.R. Schellenberg.[2] W. Benedon[3] is the leading writer on records management and wrote from the point of view of a large American manufacturing company. Reacting to the work of these authorities, the present author[4] brought out a manual of archives and records management which was based on the experience of smaller organisations, an experience which could more easily be translated to fit the needs and practices of the majority of people faced with problems in managing their records and archives. The American *Basic Manual* series also tried to take a pragmatic view, which would reflect the experience of a variety of archives services and traditions.[5]

The experience and background of all these writers led them to approach the problem of describing the administration of records or archives in basically the same way in all cases. They described the work and materials they were accustomed to, added an analysis of the underlying problems, and a superstructure of theory, and produced the whole as a kind of complete and self-justifying system. This method of treatment had the advantage, as it was perceived by most of the people involved, that it tended to emphasise the differences between archive and library techniques and systems.

Some time during the late 1950s — probably after T.R. Schellenberg's momentous tour of Australia in 1954, and certainly after the appearance of the Grigg Report in the same year[6] — there emerged a new school of archives management. The protagonists of this school, which included a number of important writers — F.B. Evans,[7] Ernst Posner,[8] M. Roper,[9] and Schellenberg himself — claimed to have perceived a new dynamism in the movement for the preservation

1

and exploitation of archives. The feeling of the time was that archive administration had been lifted away from a rather dusty and antiquarian past in which it had largely acted as a support to historical studies. Instead it had been brought into a present in which the discipline was the direct servant of current administration and of the public. In the new school of writing, emphasis passed away from the conservation of ancient materials, and from the study of historical interpretation, towards the provision of information in planning and government. The good management of current and recent records linked closely with this, ensured the inflow of new archives from modern activities, and provided large economies in records storage as well as improvements in administration. Seen against the background of modern trends in historical and social research, in which increasing numbers of researchers seek access to recent records, the modern school of archival theorists gave the necessary literary and theoretical backing to the spread of archives services and institutions which, encouraged by UNESCO[10] and the International Council on Archives,[11] was a feature of the 1960s and 1970s.

In the meantime, there had been very great developments in the world of information services. Information science came into existence as a discipline associated with a set of practices and techniques. Information science made a relatively rapid conquest of librarianship: most university and polytechnic departments of library studies changed their names to become departments of library and information studies, or the like, during the 1970s. Computers and their effects spread rapidly, and library and documentation services got used to new habits such as centralised cataloguing, and access to on-line data bases. Information management became an important aspect of the management of companies.

The spread of this movement into the world of archives was slower, because, largely for historical reasons, the training of archivists is usually in separate establishments, and most archives services of any size are managed separately and very differently from the parallel library and information services. Despite this isolation, there were influences at work, and today the world of archive administration is becoming much more open to ideas from the world of the other information services.[12] Penetration by technology is a part of the reason for the spread of new ideas, though its importance should not be over-estimated at the present time.[13]

This book is a response to the new influences, and can

therefore claim to be different. In many ways the actual practices it describes have not changed all that much from practices which were common before. It is the standpoint which has changed, and with the standpoint a profound change in attitudes and values — changes in techniques as well, which are derived from newly evaluated goals and objectives. The aim of this book is to reassess the theory and practice of archives and records management, viewing them from the standpoint of processors and suppliers of information, as part of a developed and effective information management service.

The need for such a reassessment became apparent to the present author during a study visit to Jamaica in 1983. This small country is one of the world leaders in the establishment of a planned national information system, in which the library, archives and documentation services will be developed integrally in accordance with a national plan.[14] In accordance with this development plan, the Jamaica Archives service had instituted a large-scale records management system.[15] This was to be based upon a capacious records centre in central Kingston, with a staff of records analysts who would, with a network of clerical support, manage the records produced in the various Ministries. In developing countries, records management of this kind is particularly valuable, since not only does it economise on resources, but it renders useful the information which is locked up in the files (often enough the unmanageable and irretrievable files) of government departments.[16] At the same time, the libraries which had been developed by specialist ministries were being built up to include technical documentation services. To an outsider it was strikingly obvious that the lack of close co-ordination between these two developments, records management and the specialised documentation centres, was a considerable drawback. The scheme would be vastly improved if these two strands could be brought together. The umbrella under which this could be done would inevitably be called information management.

What is suitable for Jamaica is certainly suitable for the world. It is true that at the level of major library and archive services in the developed world, institutional identity and the momentum of the past will, for good or ill, continue to preserve separatist practices. Outside these, all branches of the information industry will do well to come together, and will find that by doing so they will become more useful and better recognised by their users.

Two other signs have pointed in the same direction. At the annual conference of the Society of Archivists in 1978 a group of (mainly younger) archivists came together informally and began the process which led to the foundation of the Specialist Repositories Group. They found that a considerable proportion of the membership of the Society was now employed in archives or records services other than the traditional staple of the trade, the local authority record offices. It had been difficult for any kind of corporate recognition to grow up among the specialist repositories and their staff, not only because they are very disparate in character but also because many of them had been omitted from the principal official guide to archives services.[17] The SRG now has a vigorous programme of activities, and its appearance helped to stimulate the appearance of a totally new and comprehensive guide to archives in Britain.[18]

The second sign has been the evidence of the growing interest of museums in the collection and administration of archives. Several important museums, together with the Museum Documentation Association, have actively participated in the Methods of Listing working party, the outcome of whose work was the general structure of data elements discussed in Chapter 7. Their partnership, like those of colleagues from library services, has been a fruitful one for the development of cataloguing practices.

These, which had remained largely uncodified up to the present, came under scrutiny as a result of initiatives by the Computer Applications Committee of the Society of Archivists, and MLWP. Assisted by grants from the British Library Research and Development Department and the Society of Archivists, a research unit was set up, the Archives Description Project at Liverpool University. The project's report was the *Manual of Archive Description*,[19] which gives a detailed standard for archival description. The present book does not aim to duplicate the work of MAD, but refers to it in detail. The aim of this book is to explain the general background and setting of MAD, and to suggest ways in which these newly established standards can be integrated into a total service.

What are archives? A reassessment of the subject had better begin with its most basic definition.

The earlier writers, in defining archives, picked out two principles which they saw as the important distinguishing points. These were, firstly, that archives were media which had been generated by an organisation in the course of its business, and which had turned out to be worth keeping; and secondly, that these archives had been selected by some means or other from a larger body of media produced by the same process, which had not passed the selection test, and much of which was not worth keeping in the long term. The components of this larger group, are, in principle, called 'records'.[20]

In the light of this kind of definition, archives and records can be seen to have some properties which mark them off from materials which look similar but which are handled by different people: manuscripts and non-book materials in libraries. The important thing about archives and records is that, having been created in the course of business, it is natural that they should be administered by a service which is part of, or at any rate responsible to, the creating organisation. Every complex organisation naturally generates records and archives, and naturally also needs to manage them for its own advantage. An archives service, therefore, is an organisation which exercises these administrative functions, either within the larger organisation which has created the records, or by delegation from it.

Since libraries are organisations, they too generate records and archives; but these are not the same as the manuscripts or other non-book materials which the library may collect from external sources. Collecting manuscripts is not the same as exercising the duty of archival management, delegated by a creating organisation. There is a real distinction. Unfortunately it is one which has been exaggerated by people who have an interest (whether justifiable or not) in maximising the differences in technique and function between library services and archives services. But the distinction nevertheless is real, and has given rise to the view that the handling of manuscript materials must be divided into two quite distinct traditions, named by a recent writer[21] as the Public Archives Tradition and the Historical Manuscripts Tradition. It is one of the purposes of this book to examine and evaluate this distinction.

An impartial observer may find it difficult, in practice, to see where the difference between archives and manuscripts lies. An archives service of the PAT kind manages the records (the raw material from which it draws the archives) of its employing body. A manuscript library under HMT acquires particular items by collecting them through a more or less arbitrary system of marketing. But the materials themselves may differ less than the method by which they are acquired. On the one hand, the PAT archives may well contain items acquired originally from outside the organisation (by purchase, even). On the other hand, the manuscripts bought in by a library may exhibit archival characteristics — they may actually be the archives of an organisation which has disposed of them: in this case one may say that the library is exercising delegated functions, though the delegation is implicit. It is quite normal for archives services to exercise some at least of the functions of a manuscript (or even of a general) library; and it is quite normal, nowadays, for a manuscript library to enter into service relationships with an organisation which covers the management of archives. Though the two traditions do exist, and must be described distinctly, it is not possible to separate them in a discussion of how to manage archival materials.

Manuscripts are controlled and catalogued in ways that are governed by rules of bibliographic description generated from within the world of library science; in particular by Chapter 4 of AACR2, or by a set of instructions intended to replace it. These rules have so far been regarded as inappropriate by most archivists. One of the objectives of this book is to seek to extend the application of the descriptive methods suggested by MAD until they meet the boundaries of AACR2's effective application.

The discussion has led us to a point where we can begin to consider new definitions. As we have seen, an essential feature of archives is that they are materials acquired under some form of delegation: the archives service is carrying out functions which are natural to the archival management of the originating body. But the chain which links that body with the eventual custodial service may be obscure. However this may be, no custodian will trouble to keep an object unless it has a clearly perceived value, if possible a value which can be quantified and compared with the costs of preservation. In some cases this value resides in the physical qualities of the archives, which are intrinsically valuable as objects; but in most cases archives are kept because the information they contain is the valuable element about them. They are primary sources; and the situation of mankind is

6

such that primary sources are an essential part of the information stock. There will never be a time when a proportion of people is not engaged in researching primary sources in order to process information for more general use.

Of course, there are many different kinds of primary sources, and there are also gradations of 'primaryness', which sometimes make it hard to distinguish clearly between primary and secondary documentation. To the user, the distinction would not necessarily be of great interest. A researcher using primary materials is concerned to evaluate the trustworthiness and even the meaning of his source. To do this, he must learn the circumstances of its origin: he must know something about its custodial history. The original context is important, as are features of the document's diplomatic — significant marks on it, the formulas of its wording, or its shape and colour. The authenticity of the materials is tested by reference to these two things, provenance and format. After an evaluation of these, the only important thing about the source is its relevance to the enquiry on hand, and of this the user is the best judge. The user will select the most relevant materials for his enquiry, he will select them from all available sources, and he will subject them to tests of authenticity and validity.

It appears from this that the differences between archival materials and other information media, are of interest primarily to those who have to manage them, and much less to the users. If this is true (at least in general), two conclusions can be drawn. Firstly, the strength of the distinction which has traditionally been maintained between archives transferred to an archives service from within the organisation, and primary materials received from other sources (the distinction between official and non-official archives) may be reduced. Of course, it is still necessary to preserve a record of the provenance and custodial history of an archive, but not to insist that different sources imply different values.

Secondly, archival material can be evaluated as a source as against other sources available in the same institution. What is distinctive about the archives is their origin, not the quality of the information they carry (which may be great or little, as with other media). The definition of archives can therefore concentrate on their origin within the creating agency. Archives are information-bearing media which have been generated from within the organisation; library and documentation materials are information-bearing media which were originally acquired from outside the organisation.

A definition such as this places archives services firmly in the context of other information services. Libraries administer information held in materials bought in from outside (mainly books and journals); documentation centres manage materials also acquired from outside, but through specialist channels (mainly technical reports and papers); specialised repositories manage technically different media (such as film, videotape, audio recordings and other non-book or non-paper materials). Together these services provide, maintain and exploit the information stock of an organisation or of a community. In terms of the full information picture, each type of service is dependent on the others, and users appreciate this. It would be natural if the management practices of the three sectors could be co-ordinated, and should approximate to each other, and it would be natural if the various branches of the profession of information management should be more closely integrated in their work and in their training.

A definition which speaks of internal generation of materials still leaves unresolved the distinction between archives services which are departments of the creating organisation, and those which are external collecting agencies. At the extremes, these two types will presumably always remain very distinct from each other. The PRO will never resemble the Department of Manuscripts of the British Library much more that it does now. Nevertheless, the archival nature of much of the holdings of the collecting services gives validity to the notion of delegated archival management. Most archives services exercise these delegated powers in relation to material acquired from outside. The definition can still stand, but with one important proviso, which is that archives services may (or should) appraise the material they accept with an eye to the completion of their information holdings. Like libraries, and like documentation centres, archives services seek to acquire holdings which add up to a full and relevant information stock.

To sum up, archives may be defined as information media which have been generated from within the organisation, and the management of which has been delegated to a specialist service. The purpose of this delegation is the preservation of the materials and the exploitation of the information in them.

This definition is new, but it does not displace the older

definitions, which stressed appraisal and custody. Archives are also records which have been selected and kept because of their long-term values. Nor does it disturb the practice of archives administration or records management. This practice has an established tradition which includes a fairly well understood terminology. This should be used by practitioners, as the terms and concepts involved describe systems which have been proven in experience and which are distinct from practices common in the other information professions. Thus it is important to speak of the arrangement and description of archives, and not of their classification and cataloguing: there are important principles behind these terms.

On the other hand, if archives are perceived as belonging to the universe of information media, then the terminology and practices of information retrieval will apply to them as much as to any other information service. The new approach signalled by the new definition will have its effect by helping to incorporate archives services into the framework of information services, and by helping to introduce or develop technically similar practices in the exploitation of information.

There is one other way in which the strengthening of the information-supply concept has changed the attitude of at least some archivists to their work. This is the perception that archival management resembles other information work in obeying the basic principles of information theory. The Shannon-Weaver model of the communication process, originally developed in connection with telephony, but later applied to librarianship,[22] appears to apply just as well to archives.

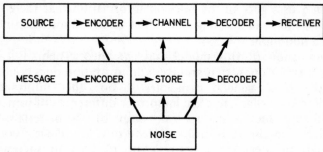

A model of the communication process within an archives service.

In this model, the assumption has been made that the source message is the archive itself. Logically, this assumption is inadequate, for the true source is the mind of the person who originally generated the material. This component has been omitted in this case, because the author of an archival document is not an author in the same way as the writer of a book. It is the event documented by the archive which is the true source, an event in which many persons probably participated, and in which the document itself had an integral part. It is simpler to begin the communication model with the existence of the archive.

The message is encoded for transmission to the receiver by the characters used in the recording process: the archive has a certain physical shape which allows it to carry the message by means of symbols. The channel is the document produced, and its passage from originator to user. The decoder is the act of reading it, an act which may involve technical interpretative skills.

Below the top line of the model appears a second, alternative, line, in which there are secondary encoders and decoders, and a store. This represents the archive service itself, which provides a second (actually the principal) channel. It carries out a second encoding, which is the finding aid system. The user has to decode this, employing whatever aids are available: specialist knowledge, guides to users, and other helps provided by the service. The finding aids are kept in a store, from which they have to be retrieved.

Noise represents any of the many factors which stand in the way of full access by the user to the original message. The most important of these is the tendency in finding aid systems to retrieve the wrong documents in answer to a request, or to fail to retrieve some of the right documents. When a user gets all the relevant information that there is in the system, and nothing redundant or irrelevant, then noise is at a minimum.

Discussion of this model and the theory behind it has shown two things: that archives administration does conform to the same general principles as do other information services; and that there are important differences of principle which are due to the special nature of the materials, the service, and the relationship of the two. If archives services should, in ideal circumstances, be planned in society in relation to the development of overall information services, then it must be accepted that they have their own resources and techniques. These must be maintained and perfected, and not subsumed in the general resources and procedures.

Succeeding chapters set out to describe and explain the practices of records and archives management, in the light of an enhanced emphasis on the provision of information as a commodity to a body of users. It is not intended to repeat well understood information, or to give a commentary on uncontroversial practices, nor is it intended that the terminology or concepts of information science should be presented in a way that will seem outlandish to managers or users of archives. As we advance into the information age, both of these will find it increasingly necessary to rely on concepts, theories and terminology which can be clearly understood within the specialist area.

To a degree, the archivists' terms of art will have to be understood also by the users. For that reason, as well as for general convenience, the term 'user' has been used, in most contexts throughout the book, in a very general sense. It includes all sorts of user, even those who are internal users — archivists who are seeking access to materials in their care, members of staff of the employing organisation who wish to access information for the support of current activities, professional researchers in pursuit of information to support a report on a clearly defined area of enquiry, and unskilled members of the public seeking relatively undefined or vague information for their own use.

2 Archives services: the background

To illustrate the nature and functions of an archives service in a national or international context, a brief survey of some of the kinds of institution concerned with archival management may be useful. Though its immediate context is that of a developed western country, and specifically Britain, an effort has been made to take into account the experience of other countries of different resources and traditions. The underlying aim is to establish a model, or series of models, which may help to sharpen the picture of what an archives service should be, and how it might be structured in order to achieve the best results.

There seem to be three kinds of institution in which archives services operate: national, local or provincial, and specialist. Cutting across the distinctions between these is another which seems nearly always to be there, that between institutions which are entirely specialist archives services, and institutions which manage other materials or share in other services as well. A second distinction is between institutions which are purely archive services, and those in which the archives service is simply a department, or represents an aspect of the work.

The National Institutions

The national archives ought in any country to be the main specialist institution in the archives field. In many parts of the world, the national archives is a unitary service, situated among the central departments of government. It will be charged with the management of government records and the passage of these through the processes which translate the most important of them into archives. One would expect the national archives to have custody of the fundamental documents of state, such as the constitution or founding charter, if there is such a thing. It would manage the most important and most central of the country's records, the records of the legislature, the cabinet or council of ministers, and the courts of law. It is from this central point that the management of the national archives spreads out through the various agencies of government.

There is an international model of how such a service might be established, the range of duties it should undertake, and the resources it would need to dispose of.[1] Based upon the experience both of developed and of developing countries, this model has been influential in forming the development plans of several countries, in respect of their archive services, and therefore there are several case studies of its specific application in particular situations.[2] These studies include specialist archives services and national information services which include an archival element.

Most European and North American countries have institutions which resemble the national archives service of the model. A good illustration of a central national archives of a modern kind, actively engaged in the management of records of government departments (albeit in this case only of Federal government departments) is the *Bundesarchiv* of the Federal German Republic. Founded only after the end of the second world war, it has established a reputation for high standards of management and for devoting attention and resources to the exploitation of its information holdings.[3] Outside Europe, another excellent example is that of the Australian Archives.[4]

Britain does not possess a good example of a national archives service on this type of model. This is a country with one of the oldest traditions of settled and continuous government, and the accumulation of archives over many centuries provides a foundation for archives work which is of great value. For this reason, the three Public Record Offices (the PRO itself, the Scottish Record Office and the PRO of Northern Ireland) began their careers with publicly recognised work in academic research, and have since retained a high reputation in this sphere. The PROs are independent of each other. They administer the records of their respective territorial sectors of government, and have developed traditions relating to their methods, the range of institutions whose records they are responsible for, and the perception of their functions and priorities, each of which is quite distinct from those of the others. The PRO is not directly concerned with the development, conduct or standards of archives services outside the strict confines of central government, although it does attempt some liaison, and some oversight of Public Records held locally. Both the Scottish Record Office and

PRONI do exercise responsibilities in the collection and use of private and local archives. In all cases there are government departments or institutions which in one way or another are exempt from the supervision of the record offices.

Legislation

The international model presupposes that the work and structure of the national archives service will be guided by legislation, and there is also a model for what this legislation should look like. A modern view is that it should form part of the legislative framework of the national information systems generally, so that it can serve as a foundation for their co-ordinated operation.[5] The materials for a comparative overview of international archival legislation are easily available, for there is a comprehensive and reasonably up-to-date digest of it, published by the International Council on Archives.[6]

The main purpose of archival legislation is to establish the national archives service and set out its duties and functions. In the case of Britain, this is done by the Public Records Act 1958, which regulates the PRO (actually founded in 1838) and sets out in broad terms the duties of the Keeper of the Public Records. He is to 'take all practicable steps for the preservation of records under his charge', and has 'power to do all such things as appear to him necessary or expedient for maintaining the utility of the Public Record Office'.[7] These things are specified only very broadly: they include making indexes and guides to records, issuing publications, regulating conditions of access, making copies of records, exhibiting them, and making special arrangements for archives which have technically demanding forms. There is no reference to any management function in this list. The PRO is placed under the responsibility of the Lord Chancellor, a senior minister of the Crown, normally a member of the cabinet, whose functions in other respects resemble those of president of the senate and minister of justice. In giving responsibility for government archives to this minister, the British government has made an odd choice, for he is neither a minister with central co-ordinating or administrative functions, nor is he the minister responsible for the nation's information or educational services, the conservation of the heritage, or the conduct of research. The post of Lord Chancellor was histori-

15

cally one which was concerned with the issue and preservation of certain central records of the Crown.

Legislation may serve to establish and co-ordinate archives services which operate in several fields: central administration, national information systems, education, conservation of the physical heritage, and research. Although in a sense the legislative background is not of primary importance (for British experience certainly shows that it is possible to run an efficient archives service, or any other kind of service, which is not suitably backed by legislation), by framing its legislation suitably it is possible for a government to decide upon and lay down lines of operation for its information services which help them in their development. Traditionally, this would have indicated that an archives law would place the national archives in a central co-ordinating or administrative position in relation to other government departments. More recently, the drift may have moved towards the co-ordination of information services. Looking at the end product in reference and research, some have considered the government department which deals with education and culture to be the proper home for the archives service. Elsewhere, other initiatives still have been tried.

In some countries, for instance, the government archives service has been placed with the principal archaeological and museum services under the direction of a minister for the heritage. In this case one would expect that activities in this area—collection, research, outreach and conservation—would be well funded, efficiently directed, and form a distinct and valuable part of the government's environmental programme

Drawing co-operative programmes together into one centrally directed service is an attractive proposition in the abstract, and may lead to substantial achievements in line with the plan. It has one defect in practice, which archivists are particularly aware of. This is that parallel services which are subject to a single direction and funding, are in effect direct competitors with each other for resources and priorities. It is often because archives services have so frequently not been part of the directorate of information or libraries (or of museums and heritage) that they have been able to secure the resources to develop fully. Nevertheless, at the present day, a reasonable view must be that the best place for the national archives is probably with the other information services. Other situations may be appropriate: the important point is that the best chance of achievement may be when

16

here is a clear goal, established by national government, and directed towards a large area of the public good, such as information, education or heritage.

It is quite common to find that some departments or offices of state are excluded from the system of management of records for which the national archives is responsible. These may often run specialist archive services of their own. This exemption may typically include the department of foreign affairs and the armed forces, both organisations which are relatively conscious of the importance of their records, and of their own independence as institutions. In Britain one of these areas of exclusion is the legislature: the House of Lords Record Office manages the archives of Parliament. Another important specialist archives service is the India Office Library and Records, dealing with the archives inherited from the colonial administration of India. There is no direct institutional link between these and the PRO, and instead, recent changes have brought the India Office Library and Records under the umbrella of the National Library.

It will be argued later that, in principle, the separate administration of specialist archives services, in certain cases, is better welcomed as a significant accession of resources, than deplored as detrimental to the tidiness of overall management by a single service. There is always more work to be done, which may be beyond the resources of one institution; and a generalist institution may sometimes fail to stimulate and support specialist areas of research as much as is needed.

Another function of legislation is to define the materials which are to be administered by a national archives service. This is done in the British case by the establishment of a category of 'public records', which are to be subject to the operation of the public records acts. Essentially, these are the records produced by central government agencies. Public records are (to quote)

> administrative and departmental records belonging to Her Majesty whether in the United Kingdom or elsewhere, in right of Her Majesty's Government in the United Kingdom and, in particular,
> (a) records of, or held in, any department of Her Majesty's Government in the United Kingdom, or
> (b) records of any office, commission or other body or establishment whatsoever under Her Majesty's Government in the United Kingdom . . .

17

A list of institutions whose records are to be included in th category is in the schedule to the act, and this list may be and has been, amended from time to time by addition c subtraction by ministerial order.[8] The possibility of amend ment in this way is a useful feature of archives legislatio

The rather narrow definition of public records has intro duced some anomalies, and cannot provide a model fc setting out the area of responsibility of a national service. O the one hand, public records are not confined to the recorc of ministries and departments of central government. Som nationalised agencies, quasi-public bodies and local agencie are included. Thus the records generated by health autho ities nation-wide are included, as are those of magistrate judges and courts. On the other hand, other similar bodie are not brought within the operation of the act, and as ha been seen, the jurisdiction of the PRO itself over the recorc of central government bodies is restricted in some areas. Th act provides that public records may be held in authorise 'places of deposit', and the PRO has a role in negotiatin which and where these are to be. Unfortunately there is litt. or no coercive power in the provision, and since the PRO h: no other co-ordinating duty, its obligation to license place of deposit remains anomalous and difficult to enforce

The Scottish and Northern Irish Record Offices deriv their existence and powers from acts specific to their coun ries, both earlier in date than the ruling English act.

A third area which should be covered by archival legisl: tion is the establishment of an access policy which will defir and protect public rights. In the period since 1945, there ha been a general tendency towards greater liberalisation c access to government archives. This received a considerab boost when the US government seized and published man series of German government papers after the war, and subs quently adopted a relatively open policy for its own docu mentation. Until the later 1970s, it appeared likely that the would be increasing liberalisation, at least in western an uncommitted countries. Unfortunately recent years hav seen a halt to the process, and a tendency towards great restriction (although this has not usually been expressed i legislation): this has particularly been the case in Britain.

It is now clear that archival legislation ought to contai provisions covering the freedom of information and dat protection. FOI is now an established principle of goveri ment operation in some countries, such as the USA, Austral and Sweden. From an archival point of view, it is important not only because it affects the public's right of access, but specifically because that right of access is extended to certain classes of current records. This in turn is likely to affect the information which is recorded in those classes, so that the control of access and the design of the record classes is a records management problem.

Data protection is the converse of this. This legislation, which is being introduced everywhere as a result of international agreements on data transfer, is designed to protect individuals from the possible bad effects of personal information about them being held on electronic data bases. The usual features of the legislation are that individuals are given a right of access to their own data, and the right to correct wrong data; data bases containing such information are to be controlled, and destroyed when their immediate purpose is fulfilled. There should be provision for retaining certain data bases as archives, for long-term research. Here too, problems of records management are created.[10]

Other National Institutions

Archives, including some which come within the category of public records, are also held by a number of other national institutions. It is natural that one of these should be the national library, one of the functions of which is to be the principal archival library, or library of record, of the country. Included in this function is usually that of being the library of legal deposit, and the main depository of official publications. Since both of these are important components in the nation's stock of retrospective information, the national library must necessarily play an important part in the overall archival services of a country.

The British Library Department of Manuscripts has a very large amount of archival material, some of it originating in the departments of central government in past times. The legislative basis of the British Library is quite different.[11] It does not have powers to administer any group of records or archives, but is regarded as a central repository for archives and manuscripts of national importance, other than those currently being generated by government departments. Acquisition is normally by gift or purchase, and its officers take active steps to discover details of any appropriate materials which might become available. The British Library Department of Manuscripts is an interesting case study, for in the past it has made a serious bid to become the national archives, and although this objective was not adopted officially, it does now employ the largest specialist staff and contain the second largest accumulation of archive and manuscript materials of any institution in Britain. Accessions continue to be either actual archives (papers originally generated by some continuing organisation, including individuals with public office) or manuscripts (individual documents of historical or research value) which may or may not once have had an archival relationship with a creating organisation.

The British Library began life as a department of the British Museum, and it is natural therefore to consider it as one of a group of prestigious national museums, all or most of which have an archival function. The National Maritime Museum, for instance, seeks to acquire the papers (i.e. the personal archive) of admirals and naval personages. The Imperial War Museum looks for the papers of military men of all ranks. The British Museum (Natural History) and the Science Museum take the archives of eminent scientists and innovators in technology. The Tate Gallery acquires the papers of important figures in the world of painting, the Victoria and Albert Museum those of more general artistic relevance. All museums have both a subject area in which they collect, and a naturally growing archive generated in the course of their research (and curatorial) activities. Archive material which bears upon their specialist subject is naturally included with the other objects to be collected. The archives which document the existing collection of objects is naturally required as part of the research material of the museum; and the archives arising from the museum's conduct of its business are naturally needed also as part of the research resources of the institution. The museum connection is certainly a most important one for archives, and spreads as much into the field of research and exploitation as into that of conservation.

Local Archives Services

Countries with a centralised national archives service have found that they may be obliged to set up provincial, municipal or local archives services, to manage the archives produced by these branches of government. In France, for instance, there are 101 *départements*, some overseas, in each of which there is a repository building, and trained staff under the direction of an officer responsible to the national director in Paris.[12] In Britain there is no such service, but since the first beginnings of the movement for the establishment of local records offices (in the 1920s) it has become accepted that an archives service should be provided by the basic local government divisions, the counties. At the present time all but a very few county councils maintain a specialist archive service, generally known (on the national model) as the county record office.[13]

Legislative provision for these services is minimal, and has always lagged behind actual practice. There is no model or standard for these county record offices, either in law or in physical resources. They normally carry out two different programmes: they acquire archives from private and non-official sources relevant to their own territorial area, and they administer the archives of the county government itself. Each of these programmes has a different legislative underpinning. The external collecting function is permitted by the Local Government (Records) Act 1962, which also allows the provision of public access and outreach facilities. The internal management function is suggested, but hardly more, by the ruling local government acts. These acts, and the general conduct of local government, are the general responsibility of the Secretary of State for the Environment. This minister, and his predecessors in comparable office, have occasionally issued circulars giving advice on arrangements for archives, but these have never been either specific or authoritative, and the responsibilities of his office do not cover any other information or educational functions. Most, probably all, county record offices are responsible for some public records, for the purposes of which they may be recognised as places of deposit, but there is no institutional link with the national archives.

In Scotland, the functions of the former counties are discharged in general by regions, several of which have established record offices. One of these, the Strathclyde Record Office, is the largest of its kind in Scotland, and compares in size and facilities with any comparable office. Some regions do not undertake any work in this field.

An anomaly exists in the areas of the major conurbations, where there has never been a satisfactory arrangement for

21

overall city government: consequently there is usually no satisfactory archive service in these areas, and the legal situation is confused. Generally this is true too of the Greater London area, where powers are shared between the Greater London Council, which maintains a record office, and some of the London boroughs, which are interested in archives work through their libraries. In other parts of England and Wales, there are a few non-county local authorities which, for local or historical reasons, maintain a public archives service, usually without any specific legal underpinning.

The anomaly of the great urban areas is one which can be perceived or suspected to exist in many other parts of the world. Fundamentally it arises from a confusion between the functions of a library service and those of a local archives service. City governments are accustomed, in most parts of the world, to provide a public library. In Britain, local library services operate (as far as the collection of archives is concerned) under libraries and museums acts.[14] Such a library often would possess a public building of some presence and character, and would have an extensive body of users. The public library is naturally interested in providing facilities for access to archives bearing upon the city and its cultural area. Urban library services therefore quite often provide the archives facilities for these areas, and it is common for them to display the disadvantages of archives services run by libraries — they are frequently run to lower professional standards (especially standards of resourcing) than those of specialist archives services — and they frequently take little interest in the management of the employing authority's own records.[15] Their tendency to cling to the PAT approach of manuscript curatorship means that traditions of active field-work and administrative liaison tend to be weak.

On the other hand, it is frequently observed that rural provinces commonly have well established archive services, based upon the provincial government authorities. These areas may typically have relatively weak library facilities. Archives services in these regions may perhaps show the opposite faults to those of the urban areas: they may neglect the collecting function in favour of the internal management of their employing agency's records; they may have relatively poor standards of reference service and user access, and may have little experience of bibliographic reference services and data bases. Rural archives services may in some respects show a tendency to usurp some of the functions of a library

22

service, building up a local collection of printed material, newspapers or memorabilia; or they may tend to usurp some of the functions of a regional museum, by collecting and displaying objects, or even sponsoring oral history or archaeological research.

These cases of confused function show not only what happens when the support and direction given by central government through legislation and regulation is missing, but also that there is a natural tendency for information services to grow together when functional needs and the legitimate demands of the user public are made plain.

The existence of the local record offices, and of their common tradition of work, never fully written out but never challenged publicly, means that certain principles have been established. One of the most important of these is that owners of archives, whether private or corporate, have a right to expect that (if they pass appraisal tests) the materials they are responsible for will be preserved and managed at the public expense. In some cases owners may even expect a subsidy in the form of tax relief when they deposit their archives in a record office. Less important, but still significant, is the practice of accepting private or corporate non-official archives on deposit (a form of permanent loan) without the owner having to relinquish ownership. Thirdly, the tradition has grown up that research into archives, except at the national centres, is connected with local studies, and has an essential territorial link.

Single-purpose Authorities

Every country possesses quasi-governmental single-purpose authorities ('quangoes' or para-statals) whose sphere of activity covers the whole geographical area of the country, or at least extends over more than one province. In Britain examples can be found from bodies such as the British Broadcasting Corporation, the UK Atomic Energy Authority, the National Coal Board, or the British Steel Corporation. (Some of these bodies are subject to the public records acts, others are not. The distinction sometimes seems quite arbitrary.) A major single-purpose authority which is at present showing signs of developing records and archives management functions, and which covers the entire country, is the National Health Service.

The traditions of archive management developed by such authorities are varied, because they naturally reflect the special problems and characteristics of their specialist field. Thus the BBC maintains technically autonomous services for written archives, sound recordings and visual recordings. Similarly access facilities, and generally the use made of the archives, reflect the different conditions of each operation. Not much has as yet been published on the work of these archives services, but their experience is potentially revolutionary.[16] It militates against the territorial tendency shown in archive development up to the early 1970s (especially when taken in conjunction with the development of archives services in specialist firms), and has added greatly to the common experience in the treatment of special physical formats.

Similar to the single-purpose authorities are the research institutes, of which there are a large number. Many are financed by one of the government-funded research councils, though these councils have never exercised any regulatory function in relation to the standards of archive work expected. It is hard to understand this feature, especially since the entire work of a specialist research institute may be directed towards the creation of an archive. For example, the British Antarctic Survey, based in Cambridge, has the function of compiling data on conditions in Antarctica. This data is managed and made accessible by the BAS archives service, but the financing, staffing and procedures of this service have grown up late in the Survey's existence, and without guidance from any central agency. Another example of a specially outstanding research institute which has developed an important archive service is the Royal Greenwich Observatory.[17]

Among research institutes the case of the universities is a special one. There are 45 of these in Britain, and although finance is channelled to them through a central agency, the University Grants Committee, there is no central direction or guidance from government. About half of the universities have developed archive services, either in connection with a research activity carried on in the same institution, or as one of the academic functions of the university, or as a means of managing their own record resources.

An example of the first type is the Centre for the Study of English Rural Life at Reading University, or the Military Archives Centre at King's College, London. The second type

24

may be illustrated by the Department of Manuscripts at Nottingham University, the Department of Palaeography and Diplomatic at Durham University, or the Borthwick Institute of Historical Research at York University. The third type is not so common, but the oldest universities, including Oxford and Cambridge, have archives departments which manage the considerable accumulations of very old archives, and a few others, including Liverpool, Imperial College, London, Heriot-Watt and Reading have records management services. The majority of university archives services are based within the university's library.[18]

The Private Sector

Recent years have seen the rapid development of both records management and archive services within commercial or manufacturing firms. Some of these, particularly those within science-based industries such as pharmaceuticals, have a close resemblance to similar services in research institutes. Such firms tend to be in close contact with each other, and the Scientific Archives Group was established to formalise liaison.[19] In other cases the archives are run in close liaison with museum functions, and may be regarded as part of the public relations activity. Elsewhere, the main function of the archives service may be to manage either the accumulated backlog of historical papers, or the recent records of the firm. Firms which have shown interest in the museum aspect include Marks and Spencer (large retail stores) and Clark's (shoe manufacturers). Management of the older archives, of which there is a considerable accumulation, is one of the main concerns of the archives service at Rothschilds (merchant banking). In some cases an important component of the archive holding is provided by the personal or family papers of the firm's pioneering founders, as at Ferranti's. The management of recent records is the main function of many, including, for example, Pilkington Brothers (plate glass manufacture), or the National Girobank.

It is natural that records management, with its immediate implications for the cost and efficiency of current administration, should be more highly regarded in the private sector than in many public repositories. It is in this area that most rapid development has occurred of recent years, and has led to the formation of the Records Management Society of

25

Great Britain (affiliated to the International Records Management Council). However in practice most business archives services care for the historical research material and attempt to keep a balance between the two sides of their programmes.

The Business Archives Council exists to stimulate and co-ordinate these activities, runs an advisory service available to firms, and an annual training course.[20]

Private Archives

This brief survey of types of archive service may be concluded by a mention of archive services which are based upon private papers. All individuals active in public life inevitably compile an archive as they go along. It has always been difficult to define the exact boundary between the rights of the public and of the individual and his family in this field. Politicians and military men are at least usually aware that the public has an interest in their material. They may decide to send their papers to join those of Winston Churchill at the Cambridge college founded in his name, or to one of the universities. There are also examples of private archive services run to professional standards. Some of these are based upon the care of ancient documents, such as the archives of the Marquis of Salisbury at Hatfield; and some hold relatively recent papers of national or international importance. An example of the second type is the archive of Earl Mountbatten at Broadlands.

The classic model of an archives service to conserve and exploit private papers of a national character is provided by the presidential libraries in the USA. These are established and endowed by individual presidents, but are controlled by law and administered by the National Archives. Each presidential library is based upon the archives of a particular president, and seeks to acquire complementary papers from the contemporaries and associates of that president. There are legal provisions which govern the relationship between the private and public papers of national office-holders, and applying the terms of freedom of information legislation to these papers.[21]

In recent years the churches have adopted the practice of setting up archives and records services to cover their own administrative needs, and to manage their historic archives. Guided in part by the rules and experience of the Vatican archives, the Catholic church is in the process of encouraging religious orders and dioceses to undertake at least the minimum work required.[22]

It may be appropriate to add in this connection that there appears to be a growing number of freelance archives and records management consultancy agencies. It is generally possible to call in the services of these to solve problems of administration or care either of the older archive material or of current records.

Since a recent survey has listed 708 archive repositories of one sort or another in Britain, and did not claim to be exhaustive, it may be guessed that there are somewhat over 800, and perhaps as many as 1000, in existence in this one relatively small (but old and crowded) country.[23] The biggest of these repositories may have a professional staff numbering as many as twenty to thirty, but the smallest (and there are many of these) will employ only one archivist, with or without clerical or administrative support. Membership of the professional association, the Society of Archivists, is somewhat over 1000 at the start of 1984.

Similar conditions, *mutatis mutandis*, may be found in other countries, except that many countries have a better regulated national service, and have established standards of operation which govern the investment made in local or specialised archive services as well as in the national archives. A good example of this is given by the Netherlands. Developing countries have a special need of efficient archives services, since so much of the documentation of their national identity, and of their stock of reference data are held in archival form.

Central Co-ordination and Direction

It was early realised that some provision must be made, even in the most decentralised state, for private and non-official archives which are of importance to the national heritage. In Britain this was recognised by the setting up of the Royal Commission on Historical Manuscripts in 1869. This body in turn established the National Register of Archives, which has operated since 1945 as a central repository of archival finding aids. Two specialised types of archives have some degree of statutory control, in that they must be registered at the HMC: these are tithe and manorial documents. Otherwise, the NRA data base is run entirely on a voluntary basis, and consequently there is no machinery for co-ordinating the format or content of the lists submitted to it. These remain a very varied collection, many thousands in number. However the HMC does publish a number of finding aids based either upon its own research or upon the material accumulated in the NRA.

Another function of the HMC is to advise government about the operation of such regulatory functions as exist in regard to archives. These include the acceptance and disposition of archival accumulations which may be accepted in lieu of tax; and the regulation of exports of archives. The Heritage Act of 1980 has reinforced these functions.

Common Elements In Modern Practice

Most countries demonstrate development of some or all of these archives services in the different sectors, usually in a form which is dictated by the constitutional and legal traditions of the place. Attempts have been made to set out theoretical models which might suggest a framework for archival development, taking into account the various tasks which an archives service might undertake.[24]

The outline of a basic structure for an archives service might appear like this:

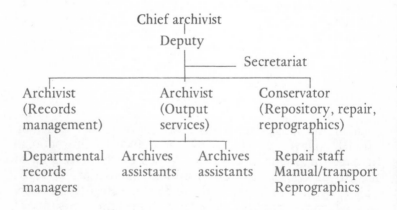

In a service of this kind there might be four categories of staff.

1.   The chief archivist, deputy and the three departmental heads would clearly be in a managerial position. Ideally, they would be professionally qualified archivists. Specialist training would be desirable in the case of records management, and necessary in the case of conservation. Some training in the skills of management is usually regarded as necessary.

2.   The staff indicated as 'archives assistants' in the model in fact carry out professional duties. It is they who process the material, that is, they arrange and describe archives, and do all the other processes needed to keep and use the material. In a large archives service, therefore, the more senior of these members of staff (at least) will be professionally qualified archivists, who supervise paraprofessionals (in this case it would be more usual to call them 'assistant archivists').

3.   In smaller archives services, the departmental heads supervise paraprofessionals directly. It is clear that paraprofessional staff (the usual designation would be archives assistants) have an essential role. Those noted as departmental records managers may also be considered as belonging to this category.

4.   Technically qualified staff include repairers (and conservationists more generally) and the specialists who maintain reprographic services. These often include microfilm, photography, various methods of printing; and perhaps microcomputers for retention and transmission of descriptive information.

The nature of the training required for each of these categories of staff has also been outlined in an international model.[25] Professional staff should be graduates who have completed a specialised training in an archive school. Paraprofessionals should be educated to the normal secondary standard, and have received a specific training: this is usually given by apprenticeship, or by in-house training courses. There is a considerable need for organised training at this level in most countries, and for a corresponding career structure. Specialist training has to be provided in specialist institutions.

There is an international movement towards the harmonisation of professional training in the main branches of the

29

information services. Although this has not as yet made much impact on the structures of existing training schools in the more developed countries, the concept of harmonisation has received a good deal of assent. Recent proposals for the foundation of new training schools, particularly in Africa, have all assumed that the three information professions would be trained together.[26] The most recent studies have produced outline requirements for common core courses in management studies, technology and user studies.[27]

The internal structure of a service. Within the service, it is necessary to delegate responsibilities. The model presented above suggests that this may best be done by dividing the processes between departments. This would certainly be the best way of delegating responsibility for technically different processes such as records management and conservation. However when the management of archival materials within the service is considered, it may prove more efficient in the long run to divide responsibility by allocating the whole management of particular archive groups to specific archivists, rather than by allocating them the supervision of specific processes.

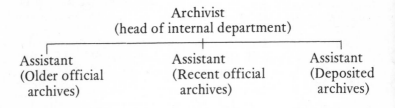

An arrangement like this would mean that each archivist would have a specialist interest broadly correspondent to a subject, and would acquire a stock of information on the activities which led to the creation of the archives in that field. Archivists need to have this kind of expertise, and the relationship with user groups which goes with it; in any case, it is a good approach to personnel management.

An archives service may have other specialists not mentioned in these models. It is quite common to have specialists in the exploitation of archival materials in school education. These members of staff may be qualified teachers, or qualified archivists, with experience in the parallel field. Other specialists may include people working on publication or copying projects.

There are some activities which are necessary components of most archives services. As in all areas of information work, it is possible to divide these activities for convenience into three fields: input, process and output.

Input

All archive services have to make some arrangement for identifying the material they are interested in, and for taking it in. So many different kinds of material are involved, that the fieldwork and accessioning systems to be found are very diverse. Examples of some of the main types of archives service are as follows:

1. A few archives services exist purely as data bases of information about archives held entirely or mainly elsewhere. This would include, for example, the Contemporary Scientific Archives Centre at the University of Oxford, and the British Political Records Project at LSE. In these projects, the main effort will be put into fieldwork, and the objective will be to create (and perhaps publish) a data base of information on relevant archive material in the whole field selected.

2. Many archive services draw their material from a territorial or subject field. Here too fieldwork is of the greatest importance, but tends to be less fully organised than in the first group. Provision for fieldwork varies from services which employ specialist staff to carry out systematic surveys, to those which virtually take no positive action to secure new material, but which are willing to accept appropriate material when it is offered by an owner or creating agency. Most archive services operate somewhere in the middle of this spectrum of activity, usually by allocating a proportion of the time of their regular staff to fieldwork. In these circumstances, it is unusual for the coverage of the fieldwork to be at all complete.

3. Other archive services may draw their material from a captive field, usually from the record systems of their employing authority. Most archives services of this type will run at least some elements of a records management programme. Here also there is a spectrum of activities. At one extreme, there will be a full records management

programme, which aims to control all the processes involved in the generation of records, the flow of records and information within the organisation, and the storage and retrieval of records and information. An example of this type of operation is BP Ltd. At the other end of the spectrum is an archives office which simply accepts consignments of records when the originating department decides to transfer them.

Many county record offices operate in this way.

Systems which operate between these extremes are quite usual. A common situation is one where the records management programme exists but is limited to control of the processes whereby records are retired from current systems and placed in intermediate or limbo record stores.

From a staffing point of view, archives services vary widely. A full records management programme demands full-time staff, whose job therefore would include carrying out the necessary fieldwork surveys. A minimal or partial records management programme may depend on part-time activity by staff otherwise involved.

There are also differences in the mechanics of accessioning new record material. A developed records management system will probably include an intermediate records store — usually called a records centre — which is an active repository for non-current records which have long retention periods. Records in the centre which pass appraisal tests may be transferred eventually to the archives. The important control point is that at which records pass out of currency and into the records centre.

Archive material should not be received or accessioned unless it has passed an appraisal test. Records management systems incorporate appraisal in their processes: indeed it is a central principle of records management that ephemeral records should be disposed of as early as possible. The archives should contain only such material as has been judged worthy of retention. Appraisal therefore must inevitably be one of the main professional responsibilities of archive staff, and it is hard to imagine an archives service, however idiosyncratic, which does not carry out this function.

Process

When received as new accessions, archive material is normally subjected to a series of processes grouped under the headings of arrangement, description and conservation.

Chronologically, the first processes are those of arrangement. In these, archivists seek, usually but not necessarily by physically sorting the material and investigating its background, to arrange the components of an archive accumulation into an order which reflects that of the system by which the documents were originally created and used. This involves arrangement rather than classification: the components of the archive are put into an order which depends on the relationship of one part to another, and not into an order which is a pre-established analysis of concepts or subjects. Archival order usually demands treatment at two or more different levels, which are determined by an analysis of the original system which created the archives, and which are treated differently in description.

Arrangement processes are completed by the physical storage of the material in containers on shelves in the repository, and by attaching retrieval labels to the containers.

Archival description is a better and more usual term than cataloguing, because

(a) the great variety of archival formats make it difficult to establish a regular system of bibliographic descriptions which would resemble a library catalogue;

(b) differences of level mean that each archives accumulation must have a compound description.

The objective in archival description may be administrative control (the control of the material through the physical processes and in storage) or intellectual control (the ultimate exploitation of the information contained in the media).

Archival conservation includes environmental as well as remedial conservation. Storage conditions should include protection from environmental hazards, and should be secure enough to ensure the survival of the archives for the period of time for which they are planned to survive: in many cases in perpetuity. Fumigation may be needed before material can be brought into storage, and repair may be necessary where newly accessioned material has been subjected to bad conditions. In some cases repair involves highly skilled craft work, in others a more mechanical process.

Standards exist for all these operations,[28] and for the buildings required for housing materials and carrying on processes.[29]

Output

The output from an archives service takes the form of usable data and the services which promote use of the materials. Generally, activities cover a range, from provision of access facilities to incoming users (passive exploitation) to the conduct of active publication, educational or outreach programmes (active exploitation). In either case, the design and completion of a finding aid system based upon archival description is necessary. Finding aids are normally published, but the outreach activity may often involve a specific programme of publication.

Output to users must be regarded as the final end of archives services, which are therefore user-oriented. This is a feature they have in common with other information services, but it is important to notice that there are two respects in which user-orientation must be limited:

(a) the input of new archival materials is determined mainly, if not entirely, by the nature of the materials generated by the target organisations. Archivists can only acquire materials which have actually been created by the organisations whose archives they are managing, even though in some cases these may be supplemented by materials collected from other sources.

(b) access to archives is regulated by statute or by some similar controls, and is based upon a considered access policy. This may be more or less liberal, but in principle there are few archives services which give totally unlimited access to their holdings.

These areas of professional activity are looked at in more detail in the chapters which follow.

3 Records management

Not all archives services carry out a records management programme, though in principle most would have the possibility of introducing one to cover the records created by their governing authority. Where an archive service has the primary duty of serving an employing authority or institution, the records management aspect is of major importance, and affects all the processes which come after it. Records management can also be considered as a function exercised independently of archival management, but the two logically go together and either may suffer from the absence of the other.

Records management is a field which has attracted increasing attention in recent times. The growing sophistication of administrative practices, and the increasing complexity of organisations, together with the enormous expansion of the quantity of records produced, has made it necessary to introduce conscious management into this area, and to develop it as a set of techniques or as a discipline.[1]

Historically, interest in records management has arisen from different points of origin. In some cases the initiative has come from archivists, whose main concern is the control of material passing out of current record systems into archival care. Records management in this tradition is concerned mainly with retirement of records from currency and their appraisal. In other cases the initiative has come from organisation and methods or management advisory units, whose main concern has been the reduction of administrative costs. In other cases again the records management system may have originated in central secretariat departments, whose main concern has been to regulate the flow of information and documentary media within the central offices. There may also be cases where records management has begun with legal advisers, whose concern has been to preserve and retrieve official documents. Finance departments have also had to develop systems to serve the needs of audit.

The historical point of origin impresses its character on the resulting programme, and it may determine where the main thrust of management effort is placed. The present study takes as its starting point the view that records management is a branch of information management. The quality of the information it supplies is the main criterion for an RM programme, and this information supply is radically affected by its relationship with an archives service.

RM is a field of management whose material is the data, media and systems used in the record-making and record-storing processes in any organisation. Its aim is to achieve the best retrieval and exploitation of the data held in these media and systems, and incidentally to reduce the cost and improve the efficiency of record-making and keeping processes.

The relationship between archives and records management can be illustrated by two models: Figures 1 and 2.

Two recent developments reinforce the validity of an information-centred approach to RM. One is the advent (more gradual than at one time foreseen) of office automation; the other is the increasing tendency of legislators to introduce specific legal requirements for record retention and access.

Office automation

A useful recent summary of developments in the automation of administrative processes has been published by a working party of the Records Management Group, headed by S.C. Newton.[2]

This investigation divides the automation of office processes into four groups: electronic data processing; word processing; micrographics; and telecommunications. Each has a distinct influence on record processing.

Electronic data processing usually involves using a machine-readable data base. From the archivist's point of view, there are two kinds of these, the accumulated and the regenerative. Accumulated data banks consist of collections of data used as a whole at one time. Regenerative data bases are constantly, or at least periodically, updated with new information, so that there is never a moment when the information is in a definitive state. Data base management systems are in frequent use today. The Newton study gives examples of integrated ledger systems, personnel records systems, automated pensions programmes, and documentation systems containing textual records. When an organisation introduces any form of data base management, it is necessarily involved in some form of administrative restructuring, aimed at assimilating the newly necessary data

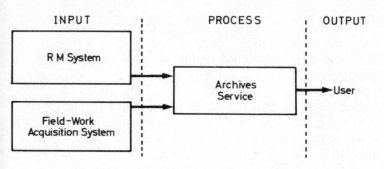

Figure 1   Records managment as a front-end system

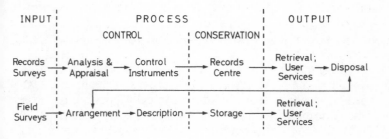

Figure 2   Records and archives management as parallel systems

processors, but also taking into account the consequences of the central data base being shared by various sections or departments.

Word processors are rapidly replacing typewriters as the main means of storing words on paper. They are inherently more efficient and flexible. When an organisation introduces word processing, it inevitably finds that it has begun a process which leads, once again, to change in its administrative structures. This is because word processors are only a small step away, technologically, from integrated electronic office communication systems. In the first stage, manually generated pieces of writing are translated into formal shapes by typing them on a word processor. In the second stage, the administrators write directly on to the word processor, which is capable of transmitting their words to colleagues or addressees, and also, if required, storing them electronically. Thus a system originally thought of as meant for formalising text ends as one for transmitting it. It will be noticed that writing and transmitting messages has always constituted a large proportion of all administrative work.

Micrographics have now developed far from their origin as storage media, into technological components of information systems. Automated retrieval of data from microforms is now advanced, either by electro-mechanical means or by using computers. Computer output is also often in microform. Recent applications include pensions records, insurance claims, purchase invoice control, and incoming correspondence.

Telecommunications is likely to be important in combination with the data transmission processes mentioned with word processors. It is already technically possible to extend these automated communication systems by means of telephone lines, and this extends into the transmission of visually read data (view-data). Together with document facsimile transmission and teleconferencing, these are developments which are likely to change the whole work environment of administrators.

All four sectors of automated recording interrelate, and all are rapidly advancing. It is interesting to notice that all concern the management of information, and the media which retains it. Whether or not we are to see the advent of a 'paperless office' (and this has been questioned), it is clear that the advance of information technology has reinforced the importance of RM as central to management planning.

An extreme view might be that in high-level administration only two kinds of managers are needed at the centre: the decision-makers, who rely on the data provided for them by the service; and the records managers, who devise and maintain it.

The design and retention of automated data bases is subject to statutory control much more closely than similar records kept in hard-copy form. Many governments, including the British, have appointed officials to supervise them, and have instituted legal codes to protect the individual. Data protection legislation is based to a great extent on international accords, and supplements the increasingly detailed requirements of law over other forms of record. Records managers must of course be equipped to observe the law in these respects, and to design their systems in accordance with relevant codes of practice.

All this shows that RM has an increasingly important role in an automated administration, and that the design of the records series to be generated, stored and accessed is a central concern of management.

Newton's study concludes with a model for the positioning of an RM service within an automated organisation: see Figure 3.

Legal control

The second recent development is that in all countries, but especially in North America and in the European Community, the law is taking an increasing interest in specifying the retention of records and in allowing litigation to be based upon record evidence over longer periods of time.

There is no comprehensive summary of these legislative requirements, which would indeed be difficult to assemble from a wide variety of statutes and legal decisions. A recent brief survey, also by S.C. Newton,[3] covering recent changes to the law of criminal and civil evidence, and of contract, is a useful guide. J. Smith's study of the law covering records of drug manufacture illustrates the importance and the complexity of the subject as it extends into technical areas.[4] Health and safety legislation has tended to specify the retention of personnel records, and to dictate the creation of records of accidents and hazards, all with long periods of currency.[5] As mentioned above, machine-readable data bases are specially regulated.

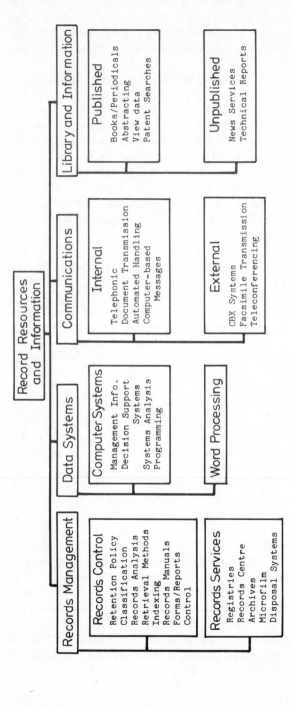

Figure 3 Possible organisation of a Records and Information Division

Source: S.C. Newton, *Office Automation and Records Management*, Society of Archivists, Records Management Group, Occasional Paper No. 2, 1981

The structure of an RM service

Records are information media which are generated by an administrative system. They include data which originated outside the organisation (for example in incoming letters), but are essentially an internal information source. Most organisations need also to provide and manage information services which seek for and use information of external origin: books and documents. No single source of information will by itself satisfy the total information requirement of any organisation, so that the RM service depends for its success on building up a workable relationship with four other facets of the organisation:

— the administration (financial, legal, general and specialist) in which the records originate;
— the special library service;
— the technical documentation centre; and
— the archives.

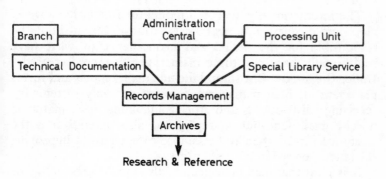

Source: Cook[6]

The *administration* generates records which carry the information it acquires and uses in the course of business. It arranges these records in systems which are the stock-in-trade of administrative departments. The RM unit must be able to build up a relationship with these administrative units which will allow the records manager a degree of responsibility for the design and maintenance of record systems, and for the disposition of particular series. The relationship should also allow the administrative departments to become accustomed to using the RM system and to call on it for information.

It is often difficult to define the concept of administration. Most organisations have a central office, the headquarters of overall management. It is common to find that there are also important administrative centres outside this. Some will be specialist or technical departments or units; others will be branches or sub-organisations, often situated away from the main administrative centre. Processing or manufacturing units also generate records, and may be administratively distinct. If it is to deal with all these, the RM programme has to be able to enter into relationships with all the different kinds of administrative entity.

The internationally accepted model for RM within government and business administrations proposes that it should be responsible for the design and maintenance of what have traditionally been the three main types of record created.[7] Under this model RM should include mail, reports and forms management. Mail management covers not only systems for receiving, distributing and storing incoming mail, matching it with mail sent out in reply, but also extends into the design of form letters and even into campaigns for improving the language used in official letters.

It is clear that mail management also involves the design of systems for filing. A filing system is essentially a practical application of a classification scheme covering the organisation's area of interest; but it also has another dimension. This is the control of movement of documents round the office, plotting a life-cycle for each letter. Incoming documents are filed, the file placed before the official who is to take action, and the resulting outgoing document takes its place next on the file. In this way a full and retrievable record is available on the whole transaction: but to set it out in this way involves a good deal of structural organisation in the office.

Reports should of course be succinct and accurately

expressed, should conform to established standards, and be available to any proper user for reference. Forms must be well designed, must make the data they carry easily usable, and (as is often remarked today) should be understood by those who have to fill them up.

The *special library service* assembles books, journals and published materials, including non-book materials, on subjects relevant to the information needs of the organisation and its staff, and runs a service based upon these. The *documentation centre* assembles published and unpublished technical papers of relevance to the organisation and its staff, obtaining these from sources outside the organisation itself, and running a service based upon these materials. An automated documentation service, common today, provides the organisation's access to international, local or specialised data bases. Clearly, reports generated from within the organisation should also be dealt with in a documentation system.

All these services may have a similar structure, consisting of input, store, and user services. The arrangements for input differ between the different services, but it is easy to suggest that store and output could be combined. In particular finding aids, systems for disseminating information, and the arrangements for communicating data have no theoretical need to be separate.

The *archives service* receives all or some of its material from the RM programme, as a result of the process of appraisal which is the interface between them. It shares with the RM programme a concern over the completeness of the documentation assembled by the system, because in the end this is what determines the value of the archive. Looked at from the other direction, the RM service uses the archives for the storage and use of its most valuable materials, over long periods.

In view of the closeness of the relationships suggested above, one could hardly suggest an RM system which does not incorporate them as an essential feature. RM systems ought to function hand in hand with the other information services.

Surveys and registers of classes

The first important job of a records manager is to find out what records are being produced by his employing organisation, and what systems are being used for their deployment.

Previous writing on RM has sometimes neglected the second half of this statement. Walk-through surveys are often recommended,[8] as an alternative to, or backed by, surveys by questionnaire. These surveys identify classes of records, and note details of these on field work sheets. This is a good way of doing a survey which notes the existence of particular records series, but it is not sufficient if the objective is to evaluate systems.

It is possible, therefore, that an RM survey should be carried out in two parts, one to establish what classes of record are being produced, and the other to determine the production processes used. The normal method in the first case would be for the survey team to use worksheets which can later be turned into a register of classes. In the second case, the survey might use flowcharts, indicating the contributory flows of manpower which lead to the production of record classes. Figures 4 and 5 refer.

Surveys of records have two main outcomes: an estimate of bulk, cost and distribution of records in the organisation; and a register of classes.

Bulk and cost

An example of the technique of estimating bulk, distribution and cost of records is provided by the work of R. Chesterman in his survey of Cheshire County Council records in 1977.[9] This included the design of summary sheets on which the findings of the survey workers, recorded on worksheets, could be analysed (see Figure 6).

Register of classes

The second essential outcome of an RM survey will be the establishment of a register of record classes. This is a basic management tool for the RM programme, and has a long-term value. The register should contain all the information necessary for controlling the retirement of non-current records, and the disposition of the class. These two functions suggest that the register should usually be based upon a description of the records at two levels at least: a description of the class as such, and a finding aid which gives access to the individual documents forming part of it.

The British Steel Corporation's RM system illustrates the use of a two-level listing[10] (see Figures 7 and 8).

Records Survey Worksheet

Department	Division Unit	Location

Record Class		Date Span
Title / Description		
Format		

Storage Accommodation		
Equipment	Shelving (lin. m.)	Volume (cub. m.)
		Spare / Unused Space (equipment)
Floor Space (sq. m.)	Total Office Space (sq. m.)	

| Frequency of Reference Proportion % | | |
| Active | Semi-Active | Dormant |

| Retention Period Proportion % | | |
| Short Term | Medium Term | Permanent |

| Accrual Rate (lin. m. per annum) | | |

| Legal Requirments | Staff Involvement | Value of Equipment |
| Notes | | |

Figure 4 A records survey worksheet
Source: Cheshire Record Office

45

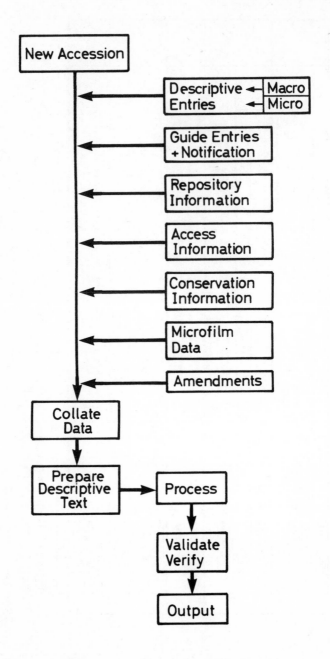

Figure 5   Data capture processes in PROSPEC

46

CHESHIRE RECORD OFFICE: DEPARTMENTAL RECORDS SURVEY - SUMMARY SHEET A | DEPARTMENT: SECRETARIAT

DIVISION: PUB. PROTECTION & MAGISTERIAL LOCATION(S): COUNTY HALL R243(540 sq.ft.) & Store(36 sq.ft.)

Date of survey: 28/4/78	Time duration: 2 hrs.	Survey staff: RGAC/ NJJ/SN	Departmental staff: Mr. J. Picking(PAA)

~~DEPARTMENTAL~~/DIVISIONAL SUMMARY

STAFF TIME INVOLVEMENT: Minimal

REFERENCE CATEGORY (% of total volume)	RETENTION CATEGORY (% of total volume) PERMANENT (a)	(b)	MEDIUM (a)	(b)	SHORT (a)	(b)	ACCRUAL RATE ft.run p.a.	VOLUME cu.ft.	SHELVING (linear ft.run)	FLOOR AREA sq.ft.	% OF TOTAL OFFICE AREA OCCUPIED BY RECORDS	% OF RESERVE STORAGE AREA OCCUPIED BY RECORDS	DATE RANGE From:	To:
ACTIVE	100%	85%	-	-	-	-	1	40	37	14½	3%	-	1910	current
SEMI-ACTIVE	23%	15%	-	-	77%	7%	MIN.	31	9	16½	3%	-	1925	current
DORMANT	-	-	-	-	100%	97%	18	864	72	36	-	100%	not applicable	

(a) = % of active, etc., records in permanent, etc., category
(b) = % of permanent, etc., records in active, etc., category

CURRENT DISPOSAL PROCEDURES:

Growth rate is minimal as correspondence files are part of central filing and Divisional records are continuously weeded of older items.

Reserve storage is entirely taken up by County Council electoral papers, which accrue every 4 years and have a statutory fixed retention period of 6 months.

OTHER COMMENTS: The Division services: the following County Council Committees: Police, Fire Brigade and Public Control, Magistrates' Courts Probation and Aftercare and the following Lieutenancy Committees: the Advisory Committee on the Appointment of JPs, the Advisory Committee on the Appointment of General Commissioners of Income Tax, and the Licensing Compensation Committee. All except the Police and Fire Brigade and Public Control Committees(Pt.I) are closed to public access.

The Division maintains close contact with the 8 Magistrates' Clerks, 3 Coroners, and Registrars of Births, Marriages and Deaths in the county, and Mr. Picking suggested that it might be worthwhile extending the Survey to include these at a future date, in the interests of continuity with the Record Office's earlier records in these fields.

Divisional summary:

REFERENCE CATEGORY (% of total volume)	RETENTION CATEGORY (% of total volume) PERMANENT (a)	(b)	MEDIUM (a)	(b)	SHORT (a)	(b)
ACTIVE	100%	85%	-	-	-	-
SEMI-ACTIVE	23%	15%	-	-	77%	7%
DORMANT	-	-	-	-	100%	97%
ACCRUAL RATE (ft.run p.a.)	1	18				
VOLUME (cu.ft.)	47	888				
SHELVING (ft.run)	43	75				
FLOOR AREA (sq.ft.)	24½	42				
% OF TOTAL OFFICE AREA OCCUPIED BY RECORDS	5%	1%				
% OF RESERVE STORAGE AREA OCCUPIED BY RECORDS	-	100%				
DATE RANGE From:	1910	1910				
To:	current	current				

Figure 6 Departmental records summary sheet

Source: Cheshire Record Office

47

RECORDS TRANSFERRED TO RECORDS CENTRE	
Part I : Data Sheet	Consignment
Originating Dept:	
	Date

General Description of Records Class

(continue on separate sheets)

Storage accommodation cleared
Filing cabinets
Transfer boxes
Shelving
Cubic footage of records transferred

Recommendations for retention

Classified   confidential / unrestricted

Transferred by

Figure 7   Part 1 of a records transfer list, giving a group/sub-group level description, and peripheral facts on bulk, storage and format

Part II : Transfer List					
Originating Dept			Consignment		
			Page		
				Records centre use	
Ref.no.	Title / description		Span Dates	Action Date	Location

Figure 8 Part II transfer list, giving an item list

Where the RM system is automated, as with the ARMS system at Tyne and Wear Metropolitan County Council, it has been found convenient to give each record class a registration number, which will uniquely identify it within its department of origin.[11] Although the ARMS system is now well established, generally most records managers would probably prefer to use free language titles for their classes. Office staff are accustomed to use a particular name for the series they create and service, and it may be better not to introduce unaccustomed technicalities.

The register of classes allows the records manager to maintain control over the whereabouts and use of the various series in his organisation. By it any class can be located, and it can be used to moderate periodic transfers out of the current records system into the records centre or into the archives, extract data when required, and advise on system changes. The most important single function of the register, though, is to construct a retention schedule.

The retention schedule

A retention schedule is an analytical list of records series, arranged either under functions or under the structural headings of a departmental organisation plan. The main purpose of the schedule is to record the appraisal decisions which have been made, so that these decisions can be put into effect routinely. A secondary purpose may be to set out the record classes in a way which will illustrate the organisation's record activity.[12]

Retention schedules usually list series by title, and note the periods during which they should be retained in the department and in the records centre. These schedules are apt for inclusion in data base management systems, and in automated systems the expiry dates can be automatically implemented.

Establishing and maintaining the retention schedule is one of the main tasks of an RM programme. In drawing it up, the records manager may take the opportunity to consult as many executives in the organisation as possible, but the final responsibility for the eventual retention decisions should rest with the RM service. This important principle is illustrated by an examination of how appraisal decisions are made and implemented.

Drafting the schedule

The register which results from RM surveys can be used to provide an alphabetical list of record classes, arranged under the departments of origin. Each of these can be allocated a proposed retention category: permanent or indefinite retention; destruction after the lapse of a given period; or review after a given period.

Proposals made in this way for retention periods can then be circulated to all relevant staff in the organisation, indeed a wide circulation and discussion is recommended. It should be made clear by what date or on what occasion replies or comments should be received. Comments by originating departments will normally be accepted and incorporated into the schedule, though if they seem perverse some further discussion should be initiated. For example, if it seems that a wholesale retention for long periods is being suggested, the records manager will be able to cost the effect of this course of action. Appraisal decisions should always be taken in the light of specific costings.

After the lapse of the agreed discussion period the retention schedule is finalised and promulgated as an item of official policy. Since schedules can and should be regularly revised, policy can always be modified in the light of experience.

Appraisal

The central professional activity of archivists is the evaluation of record classes to determine their most appropriate retention period. It is an activity built into RM programmes, for planned retention and disposal is essential to effective RM. Purely within a context of RM, the main concern of the records manager is to see that those records are retained which are specified by the law, or which are judged to be of clear administrative value to the organisation; and to see that all other records are disposed of. The archivist has a broader viewpoint, and must also consider potential research values in the records. Archivists are trained to perceive these values, and because they are participants in relevant research activities, should have acquired experience which will reinforce their ability to perceive these values. Because they involve important decisions which bear upon all aspects of the organisation's work, appraisal judgements should be made after extensive consultation, but it is the business of the archivist and the records manager to see that they have been made and that they are implemented.

It is a fundamental rule of records management that no record class should be permitted to continue without an appraisal status, and above all that no record should enter the storage system without a specific, dated, disposal instruction. Similarly, it is a fundamental rule of archives management that no document or series should be admitted to the archives without having undergone an appraisal. In both cases, retrospective appraisal, or a periodic reassessment of retention criteria, may be valuable, or even necessary. The criteria for appraisal at the two stages, in RM and in archives, are somewhat different, and this difference has been recognised in the RM practices of central government in Britain.

The system used in this context is based upon the recommendations of the Grigg Report of 1954, and was evaluated in the Wilson Report of 1981.[13] The central principle of this system, as it has been developed over the years in the management of public records, are as follows:

(a) as many classes as possible should be dealt with under a retention schedule;

(b) classes which must be reviewed are examined at two separate points in time. The first review, carried out within the first five years after closure, seeks primarily to determine whether there is a continuing administrative value. The second review, ideally at 25 years, asks whether there is also any research value.

(c) particular instance papers* are registered separately, and should have a retention instruction incorporated into their initial design.

The Grigg system outlined above depends on the validity of one central principle, that there is a broad correspondence between research values and administrative values. It is unlikely that records which are not seen as being useful for business reference will turn out to contain data of long-term value; equally material of long-term value will tend to be contained in records which are felt to be of continuing reference use. There is a convincing practicality in this view, and it has not been seriously challenged in subsequent commentary.

*Series of records each of which documents a particular instance of a general policy or activity; e.g. case files.

The Grigg Report did however note that the first review should be carried out soon after the records closure, or there would be a danger that inaccessibility would affect the administrative value judgement. It was also noted that where a record class arose from a function which had been discontinued, there would be no administrative value in the records (except possibly as a precedent), and therefore a judgement would have to be made on research grounds. One might also note that central government can make assumptions which are questionably relevant to the situation of other types of administration. One is that considerable lapse of time is needed to determine research values, and that documents must be archived only when they are thirty years old. Another assumption not universally valid is that all records will be organised in orderly registry systems, and that appraisal is a function end-on to the registry.[14]

The Records Centre

Records in fully current use must of course be kept where they are most convenient to their main users. It is one of the principal functions of the records manager to see that records which have passed out of full currency are regularly retired from these current systems, and that for the remainder of their agreed life they are managed in a suitable place. It is normal for an RM system to have such a place, known as the intermediate records store, or, more usually nowadays, the records centre.

Records centres have been in use in larger organisations for up to forty years, and a good deal of experience has been accumulated on them. There are specific standards for their physical characteristics, and for the services which they should provide.[15]

Experience has shown that there are two broad categories into which records centres fall, and that there are important record series which cannot be administered in records centres at all.

In-house records centres are generally connected with smaller organisations, with compact central administrations in confined quarters, or with RM systems confined to a few central departments. These records centres will tend to be in relatively high-cost accommodation, and will tend to be cramped for space. The space problem is usually so important in these circumstances that it is not unusual to have off-site supplementary records centres for less actively used material. Retrieval of records from in-house records centres will be rapid, with document delivery perhaps after only a few minutes, and the RM staff will have a relatively intimate acquaintance with the systems in use in the administration served.

It is common for RM programmes to start out with in-house records centres, and use them to establish trusted services for senior management or central administrative departments. When these are well established, the RM programme can expand to include services to production departments, outlying subsidiaries or branch installations. This kind of expansion will have to be accompanied by expansion into off-site records centres.

Off-site records centres are needed by larger or scattered organisations, or where the parent organisation is confined to high-cost premises in a city centre. The off-site records centre is a low-cost, high-density store, situated in an accessible but remote site. Retrieval of records from it will be relatively slow — perhaps a 24- or 48-hour delivery service, using public means of transmission or transport, might be envisaged. The selection of records for transfer to the records centre is obviously affected by the delivery delays, though the appearance of electronic document transmission systems may be beginning to affect this.

Generally, RM programmes have to deal with such a large bulk of records that some sort of off-site records centre will become necessary. All RM services should of course be costed. It will be found that central management of records, allowing early retirement of records from costly central storage, will always provide economies, sometimes very significant economies, as against systems which retain non-current documents in prime sites. To maximise these economies the full benefit of cheap bulk storage should be used. Rapid retrieval is certainly an important consideration, but the cost of providing it in particular cases may be weighed against the certain and heavy cost of keeping a large bulk of records in high-cost areas.

Records unsuitable for records centre treatment The concept of the records centre is that it should be the best environment for all records which have a retention value longer than that of immediate currency, and which do not have to be kept in prime office space. This definition covers the great majority of records other than those in full currency. There are however cases where an important record series with long retention value is still required to be kept near work stations. A typical example might be a central personnel record which has been miniaturised or automated. A personnel record in microfiche (more probably microjacket) forms, in effect, a central archive which can be housed in a fireproof safe in the principal offices. The process of archiving could if required include a security duplication of the series elsewhere (in the archives).

Other cases of the same sort are classes which receive a regular accrual at intervals. If these are brought into the records centre, the records manager has a difficult choice: the successive accruals may either be given new locations, which means that it will be difficult to find any given record; or they will have to be integrated into a single series at periodic intervals — but this is wasteful of space and labour. The solution may be to miniaturise the class, and keep it near the use point.

A third example can be taken from medical case records, where it may be necessary to provide virtually instantaneous access even to records which have been unused for some years. Microforms may be unacceptable owing to the need to have a reading machine appropriately sited. A solution may be to retain a special series near to the point of access.

There are also cases where it may be efficient to exclude certain branches or departments from the records centre service — for instance where retrieval would be exceptionally costly. Situations like this are unfortunate, since they expose defects (perhaps necessary in the circumstances) in the design of the RM system. The danger is that defects like this may be so serious that they lead to *ad hoc* or rival RM practices growing up in separatist departments. To avoid this danger records managers need to build in compensating features, and take special measures to maintain control over the records systems in awkwardly outlying departments.

These cases where certain classes of record appear to be unsuitable for management in a records centre illustrate the dispersed responsibility of a records manager, who must understand the needs of the user, and be able to design records series which do not conform to standard procedures.

In general, however, the records centre is a tool which allows records managers to establish physical control over most records which are to be retained beyond currency, and to organise them to provide the best possible reference service.[16]

Inflow of record materials

No record should enter the records centre unless

(a)   there is a retrieval instrument controlling it; and
(b)   a disposal instruction has been set up to provide for its appraisal and ultimate removal.

Failure to observe either of these rules will lead to important failures in the system.

The usual control instrument in records centres is known as a transfer list, for which there is an established model.[17] It is a curious fact that RM systems usually depend on these lists being made out by the originating department.[18] This custom, which is based on central government practice in Britain and the USA, has the advantage that it reduces the costs of the RM programme itself, by shifting a significant burden on to the originating departments. It is anomalous in that it is the RM staff who have the expertise to list and index records, and that if others are to do this work, there must be close supervision. On the other hand, the staff of the originating departments have the best knowledge of the content and use of the classes they are describing. It would be foolish to suggest that such a deeply ingrained tradition should now be changed. However there are serious defects in the make-up of traditional transfer lists, considered as instruments for intellectual control of the materials.

The main need is for a description of each record *at the appropriate level*. This means that in most cases, if not in all, there will have to be two different descriptions at two different levels. Ensuring that this is done will certainly involve the RM staff in some descriptive activity. Secondly (this is already well recognised), the description given to each record must correspond both with the title normally given to it by its originating office, and to its actual content: thus, it will be possible to retrieve the record either by its customary name or as the result of a subject enquiry. Thirdly, the retrieval system must have some means of entry into the accumulated bulk of transfer lists. These three points will be dealt with in turn.

1. Multi-level description.   This question has already been tackled in connection with the register of classes. The example given there shows a two-level description of a

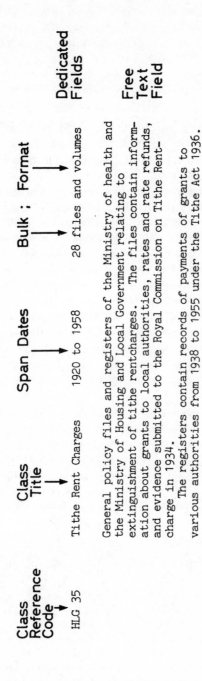

Class Reference Code	Class Title	Span Dates	Bulk ; Format	Dedicated Fields
HLG 35	Tithe Rent Charges	1920 to 1958	28 files and volumes	

General policy files and registers of the Ministry of health and the Ministry of Housing and Local Government relating to extinguishment of tithe rentcharges. The files contain information about grants to local authorities, rates and rate refunds, and evidence submitted to the Royal Commission on Tithe Rentcharge in 1934.

The registers contain records of payments of grants to various authorities from 1938 to 1955 under the Tithe Act 1936.

Free Text Description

Free Text Field

Figure 9 A class description

Source: PRO Crown Copyright, reproduced by permission of the controller of H.M. Stationery Office

57

series, at class and item levels. To ensure control of the information within materials entering the records centre, the levels should be moved downwards to provide as much detail as possible at both levels. Class descriptions may be based on the register of classes. Figure 9 demonstrates a class description, consisting of a free text abstract and five dedicated fields.

2. Customary titles.   The use of customary titles is very ancient. Documents such as the Black Book are quite familiar to students of the middle ages. Since the term 'Black Book' is valuable for retrieval only if the external physical appearance of the document is the main characteristic sought for, some further description is necessary. In this particular case, this has been provided by a published edition.[19]   The original customary name is still necessary, though, not only because it is called by this in the originating department (until it becomes an ancient relic) but because it has probably been cited under this name in published research work. RM staff have the continuing and essential duty of ensuring that document descriptions always match the contents of the documents.

3. Means of entry into the finding aids.   Large RM systems customarily limit their problems of document retrieval by referring these problems back to originating departments. These departments are given a copy of the transfer list at the time of the records' transfer. If they wish to consult their records, they must scan their file of transfer lists and specify the document they need, together with its location code. The RM staff are then only responsible for identifying the document and issuing it: their responsibility is only of an administrative kind, and therefore they only need finding aids which give administrative control. Originating departments, of course, may construct indexes if they wish.

This system has the additional advantage (from the point of view of the RM staff), that it reinforces the security of the records. Since they can only be retrieved by way of a request from the originating department, that department is clearly solely responsible for controlling access to it.

However, the narrowness of the principle operating here becomes obvious as soon as the overall interests of the employing organisation are considered. This organisation presumably runs an RM programme so that it can exploit the information held in internally generated media. The RM programme employs staff trained in information management; the originating departments employ staff trained in the product or function of those departments. To force departments to be totally responsible for record retrieval (both in the original listing and in the identification of documents to be searched) could be regarded as an abdication of responsibility on the part of the RM specialists.

This critique becomes more powerful when the finding aid itself (the transfer list) is examined. Though it gives reasonable administrative control, it is not well designed for intellectual control. Therefore if the RM service is to be regarded as managing information, rather than physical documents, some better finding aids will have to be designed. It will also be necessary to define the extent of the service's responsibility for the provision of information, as opposed to the provision of specified documents.

Improving the transfer lists may involve increasing the depth (or fullness) of information provided there. This may apply where series of correspondence files are concerned, or where technical reports are embedded in other records. In other cases, increased depth of description may not be possible. This must be a matter for specialist RM staff to judge. In any case, some form of index to the transfer lists will certainly be necessary. This may well involve the records centre staff in the necessary infrastructual work of making vocabularies or thesauri, corresponding to the work of the organisation.

Processing record materials

Physical care of the records in the records centre It is important to maintain a physical distinction between the records centre and the archives. Cost limitation remains important in RM, and storage conditions must reflect the fact that the RM service's responsibilities are limited to storing the records for a limited (but possibly still long) period of time. On the other hand, the records in the centre contain some which are particularly sensitive, and they should be kept securely. This suggests that the building should be decent, but not lavish. A clean, orderly warehouse gives the best model.

It is traditional in RM that the location of records in the records centre is arranged on random access lines. Boxes are given random shelf locations which are keyed to the finding aids. This method is obviously convenient and saves space, and in addition it adds to the security of the records. Boxes are anonymous in appearance, and have nothing written on the outside except the brief location code. On the other hand, records stored in this way do not display any of the relationships created by their original system or arrangement. They cannot be accessed by browsing, and it is not possible to concentrate any particular department's records in one area. Random access storage can only be operated — in full, at least — where the RM service has full operational control over the storage area. It is incompatible with any strong concept of departmental ownership of the records.

Output: exploitation and disposal

Records centres have two forms of output: the retrieval and exploitation of information; and the outflow of records under the terms of the retention schedule. These are of unequal value, but both present technical difficulties.

The question of responsibility for the retrieval of information, and its influence on the design of finding aids, has already been discussed. There remains the question of provision of access facilities. Experience shows that provision should usually be made for some degree of access on site. Originating departments may need to access large amounts of their records, and it may then be better for them to send staff to the records centre rather than to arrange for mass movement of materials. The RM staff must always be alert to the possibility that research access by external authorised persons may be required, and even that such access ought to be stimulated in some cases. Either way, searchroom facilities, backed by copying facilities, will be needed, including searchroom supervision.[20]

Close liaison between the records centre and the documentation centre may suggest that an SDI programme may be feasible. If so, record descriptions in the transfer list must be capable of acting as abstracts, and should contain the necessary keywords for profile matching.

Records series which are to be reviewed should be brought up at the appropriate date. The records manager needs to set up a system for reviewing, and for implementing the findings of the review. Ideally, reviewing should be done by RM staff, who should forward their recommendations on retention or disposal to the senior management of the originating depart-

RECORDS CENTRE

To   [Department of origin]

Disposal of records

The records listed below have now been reviewed in
accordance with the official retention schedule. This
class has been issued on request ..... times scince
transfer. It is recommended that :

a)   they should be transferred to the Archives and
     retained permanently;

b)   they should be retained for a further period and
     reviewed again after...... years;

c)   they should now be destroyed.

[strike out if inappropriate]

If you agree with these recommendations, you need
take no action. If we do not receive any comment by
the end of next month, the action proposed will be
carried out routinely.

Date   Signature

Reference	Description	Dates	Location

**Figure 10   A review report form with recommendations for
disposal**

Source: Liverpool University Archives

ment. This can be done on a review report form, such as is shown in Figure 10.

This method of review minimises the movement of records, and avoids the difficulties and delays involved whenever this responsibility is dispersed. It may not be feasible in very large organisations, in which specialist knowledge of particular functions is needed. In these cases, the situation to be avoided is one where the most influential advice on retention is given by people who are remote from the responsibilities and costs involved in records retention. Relative cost is always an element in appraisal, and so too is relative frequency of reference. On both these points the RM staff are likely to be the most aware of the facts.

Transfer of records to the archives should occur where records are specified as being for permanent retention. In the archives they can have a more carefully controlled environment, and entry there will provide the opportunity for a more refined retrieval system. Because of these factors, there is often a case for transfer to occur at a relatively early date. In central government the statutory principle is that transfer should occur when the selected records are thirty years old, at which period they become available for public access. In other situations, for instance in business firms, the whole concept of public access at a particular date may be questioned. Early transfer to the archives may then allow for access by specially authorised users at any date, and will provide better for conservation as well as retrieval.

It often happens that there is no physically separate archives repository, and the records centre has to perform both functions. This doubling up may have some advantages. For instance it may be useful to keep some important series which are scheduled for archival retention in a single centrally available place. In other ways the different functions of the records centre can only be reconciled with those of the archives with some loss. Typically, this will be a loss of environmental and conservational conditions.

It is established in Britain and in most advanced countries that records which have been appraised as appropriate for archival treatment can be deposited in a publicly financed archive repository, and administered there free of charge. There are no universally applicable conditions, even as to eventual freedom of access, but there is a tendency today for restrictions to be introduced on the right of owners to withdraw deposited records after a period during which they have been maintained at public expense.

Some records series have to be retained in the records centre for long or indefinite periods, but are not scheduled for eventual transfer to archives. These may include personnel records (which must be retained in some form up to and beyond the period of service of the persons concerned — say up to sixty years), and case files (which may have an indefinite closure date dependent on some external event not notified to the RM staff). The existence of these may affect the standard of storage conditions given in the records centre, and will certainly affect the calculations involved in predicting the amount of record storage needed in the planning period ahead.

Automation In Records Management

In the field of RM, successful automation so far has concentrated on providing a streamlined version of manual administrative control. System-generated information provides somewhat better guides to bulk, location, issue control and measurement of use than is common in manual systems, but so far there seems no tendency to use automation to improve information retrieval. In particular, there seem to be no on-line searching or machine-generated indexing systems operating under the label of RM.[21]

Bartle and Cook's survey[22] gives details of two well established RM systems in use in county councils. It also notes that newly developed systems tend to be ones which control both current and non-current records, that is they are not systems simply for the control of records centres. RM automation is now looking not at the possibility of automating transfer lists, retention schedules and the circulation control of records, but at the control of registries or central filing. Further advances in automated systems for RM must probably await the development of automated systems for administration and office processes, as mentioned at the start of this chapter.

4   Acquisition and archival appraisal

Up to this point, appraisal has been treated in the context of RM, in which the main considerations are administrative value and legal requirements. However the international standard for a training curriculum in archives and records management, places the subject of appraisal clearly within the area of archival management and not in that of RM.[1] This (to some, eccentric) determination suggests that there is more to be said about the acquisition of archival materials, the assessment of the information within them, and the principles behind an archival appraisal programme.

One of the most important activities of an archives service is the delimitation of its field of activity. One naturally assumes that this question might be cleared up at the time when the service was first established, and its aims decided upon. Many archives services would find it useful to bring the matter into discussion again at suitable intervals, perhaps at the time of their annual report. Things change; new needs are perceived, new absences are spotted in the network of coverage nationally.

It is useful to think of the service's field of activity not only in terms of materials but also in terms of subject, or information, coverage. The relationship between these two approaches is interlinked. An archives service exercises its interest in subject information by obtaining delegated powers and duties over the records of certain organisations, or by running an RM programme within certain organisations. There are therefore two distinct ways in which the assessment of materials for input to the service can take place: by collection and deposit, or by management. In both cases, appraisal must be a part of the acquisition procedure.

Figure 1 shows the function of RM as a front-end to the archives service. The remainder of the chapter explains how RM procedures are used to determine what records are being created and kept, and how they are appraised to determine retention periods.

There is an important difference between the aims of RM and archives administration. RM sets out to control and exploit the information which happens to be contained in the record materials and systems produced by the employing organisation. Its value as an information service must always be limited by the boundaries of that information, or by the nature of those materials. Any deficiencies in the information stock that results may perhaps be made up by liaison with special libraries or documentation centres. But in the end, if the organisation excludes from its recording work the media which carry a significant area of information, then the RM programme will not be able to provide access to that area of information.

In the case of archives, however, there is a much wider freedom to establish information-directed goals. This is true even in the case of the archives services which are closely connected with specific employing organisations, or which are responsible for RM programmes. For example, in the British context, the Public Record Office, ordinarily regarded as limited to the management of narrowly defined public records, is still evidently prepared to accept important groups of archives from outside central government, if those groups are judged to be of national importance, and to be relevant additions to the stock of central government archives. In other countries, the national archives may have the objective of assembling an archive of materials dealing with any important aspect of the national life, or at least of publicly organised aspects of it. Consequently it is common for national archives services to accept and even to seek, non-official archive accumulations, if they are judged to have relevant informational values. It can perhaps be concluded that there is such a thing as a national archives policy, which aims to compile, in one institution or in several, a data base composed of archival materials, giving subject coverage of national affairs as complete as possible.

Local and specialised archives services, and libraries and museums, naturally play a part in the overall national archives policy. The specific programmes and objectives of archives services, in the field of acquisition, are therefore information-directed. They seek to build up banks of information which will cover their chosen field of operation, and ideally that field will have some sort of link with a national plan.

Choosing its field of operation is the first serious difficulty encountered by an archives service. Despite talk of a national archives policy, there is a tradition of freedom of action which at times resembles a free-for-all. The good side to this is that where many institutions compete to provide a service, one result is an accession of new resources. This is good because in fact the total job is too big for any one institution. The bad side, of course, is that excessive and uncontrolled competition leads to unnecessary duplication, and perhaps to the scattering of materials which should be kept together. There ought to be a framework of co-ordination which maximises the usefulness of the overall bank of resources, but minimises wasteful competition. Such a framework could aptly be provided by a central agency, such as a national register of archives, armed with executive powers but working with the trust and co-operation of archivists within the country.

In Britain the NRA lacks statutory powers, and the resources to do much active co-ordination in the face of a tradition of the autonomy of archives services. There have been efforts to establish a broad agreement by informal means, but these have had limited effect.[2]

Informal co-operation between archives services, aided by the professional associations, has indeed improved over the last couple of decades. Cases of virtual piracy which once occurred when important or striking archive accumulations became available have largely disappeared, and only tend to recur where new archive services are generated by institutions which are outside the tradition of debate and consultation developed by the archives profession. A wider knowledge of the issues would be desirable.

The aim of any archives service, within its own agreed field of operation, would be to build up holdings which contain a balanced documentation of the chosen subject area. To achieve a final adequacy these holdings may have to be supplemented by information derived from the holdings of other services, including library and documentation services: this may be achieved by the transfer of materials, but more commonly by participation in jointly planned finding aids.

The most successful subject-oriented archives services have always been those which have employed full-time staff to do the field work. The task of these archivists would be to identify all possible sources of relevant accumulations, track down their whereabouts and get access to them for the purpose of inspection and (if relevant) transfer. It is not usually feasible to ask archivists who are fully engaged on other, internal, tasks, to take on this aspect of the work as well. Consequently, where there are no full-time fieldwork staff, acquisition of materials from a defined external field tends to be haphazard.

Many archival field projects are aimed at discovering materials in a defined field, but not at acquiring them. Such surveys can build up a data bank of information about the materials they find, and can perhaps do something to encourage their deposit in relevant repositories. Their main purpose remains distinct from questions of custody and access.

Archival Appraisal

It was recognised in Chapter 3 that there had to be some awareness of research values in those carrying out appraisal for the purposes of an RM system. These values could best be provided for in the system of reviews which are part of most RM programmes.

The Grigg report, operating mainly in the context of central government departments, set up a system for regular reviews. Under this, the working principle of the reviewing bodies was that there is a close relationship between current administrative values and continuing, or future, research values, but that the processes of determining these can be clearly distinguished. In selecting for preservation classes which have clear administrative (including legal or financial) values, the records managers were probably also selecting the majority of records which would eventually turn out to be wanted for the archives. The objective of the writers of the Grigg report, and of the system which was ultimately set up in the public records acts, was to find a way of shifting the administrative burden of appraisal from the archivists to the administrators.[3]

The main reason for the adoption of this principle was doubtless pragmatic. The size of the archives staff, and their logistic support, is never large enough to do the full task. Archives services are seldom perceived by Treasury officials as being central to the continuance of government service. The decision was taken to shift the main burden of archival work on to the originating departments, while encouraging these to adopt RM programmes. The departments were not directly recommended to appoint archivists, but the Inspecting Officers appointed by the PRO were intended to allow an archival viewpoint to be expressed at times of review decisions.[4]

A contrary course was adopted by NARS. Here, the task

of management of records in the Federal agencies was undertaken by staff directly employed by the national archives. In consequence NARS in its best years had relatively a much larger staff than did the PRO. The size of the staff was justified by the fact that many of them undertook RM duties, which were of direct value to the economic and efficient conduct of business. It might be thought that this was in principle a better approach than the British one, since it allowed professional judgements to be made by professionally qualified people. Experience has shown, however, that this system too has its defects. When recession came, arguments of economy and efficiency were discounted either on the grounds that ultimately the archives are a cultural and not an administrative service; or on the grounds that it would be more efficient for the managers of current records to be employed by the record-creating agencies themselves. There is truth in both these arguments, but resulting changes have tended to be to the disadvantage of the archives service. On the one hand it has had to suffer the severance of staff with current RM responsibilities, and on the other, it has tended still to be institutionally subordinated to the demands and structures of current administrative oversight.[5]

In view of the American experience, it should be possible to compare the success of the delegation approach (as in the Grigg system) with that of the direct operation approach. Unfortunately there have been no comparable studies in the two countries.

The record of the British government in the area of reviewing and appraisal was the subject of an evaluation in the Wilson report in 1981.[6] The tone of this report was determined by the view taken by the committee, that no proposal which involved new expenditure was likely to be successful; the committee also ignored pressures to improve public access to government-generated information. The resulting report found defects in the selection process, but has been criticised as being subservient in tone. The PRO, acting through its small staff of Inspecting Officers, has had great difficulty in making appraisal at all uniform, and in making it operative in all the main departments of government; in fact, there is a general impression that government departments are able to hide the truth in awkward cases, and also sometimes allow uncontrolled destruction of records.

The Grigg principle that appraisal should be delegated to the originating departments derives from a point of high principle which is peculiarly English, and was enunciated in the writings of Sir Hilary Jenkinson. This influential author considered that neither archivists nor researchers should be involved in the appraisal process. This should be done solely by administrators, who would take into account only their own administrative needs. The point is that appraisal should be impartial: the historical record should reflect the biases and idiosyncracies of the administration of the day, and not those of the academic researchers of that time, or of a later time. Of course Jenkinson was right in this, and the phrase in which he recorded his judgement has a fine ring about it:

> for an Administrative body to destroy what it no longer needs is a matter entirely within its competence and an action which future ages (even though they may find reason to deplore it) cannot possibly criticise as illegitimate or as affecting the status of the remaining Archives; provided always that the administration proceeds only upon those grounds upon which alone it is competent to make a decision — the needs of its own practical business; provided, that is, that it can refrain from thinking of itself as a body producing historical evidences.[7]

Archival appraisal certainly should be done with impartiality; but as Jenkinson tacitly admitted in the parenthetic qualification, it should be done with expert knowledge. The knowledge required is that of someone who can represent the interests of research to the world of administration; and who can represent the needs of administration to the world of research. This is a definition of an archivist. In any case, it is clear that archivists are themselves administrators.

The principles behind the American approach were laid down by T.R. Schellenberg.[8] This analysis, like Jenkinson's, perceives that there are primary and secondary values in records. Primary values are the ones which the administrators had in mind when they created the record; secondary values are those other values, such as research values, which might eventually become apparent. This looks very like the Grigg distinction between administrative and 'historical' values, and though Schellenberg's perception of administrative practice was not close to that of Jenkinson's, most archivists may accept this correspondence in practice, as a useful rule of thumb.

Archival appraisal centres upon the secondary values. In

Schellenberg's system, these are now subdivided into 'evidential' and 'informational' values. These two terms of art, although now fairly widely accepted and used outside NARS, still remain rather opaque. This terminological difficulty may suggest that the words do not strictly correspond with real concepts.

Certainly there is something suspicious about the first of the two terms, evidential. Evidential values attach to records which give evidence as to the origin and development of the organisation itself: therefore the records of evidential value are the ones which spring to prominence when the origins and administrative development of an organisation are being studied. These are the subjects which are useful for writing structural descriptions, traditionally the stock-in-trade of archivists. Descriptions like this depend on the archivist's ability to establish and write down the administrative history of the organisation he is working on. The training of an archivist, in most countries, also depends considerably on learning national administrative, institutional or legal history. From this we can see that evidential values correspond very closely to one of the archivist's main professional preoccupations. Is it possible to conclude that an archivist's tendency to preserve, first of all and perhaps mainly, the materials for the institutional history of an organisation, is based upon a delusion, and that they should be concentrating instead on identifying and preserving records which give useful information on relevant subjects? These would be documents which belong to the alternative category, and have informational values. Such a view might be reinforced by the fact that, unlike the 'evidential' concept, this one is easy to understand and remember.

If records contain information about subjects external to the evidences of the creating agency, they have informational values. These values should be substantial: they should belong to records 'contributing substantially to research and scholarship in any field of knowledge'.[9]

The registers of a company's shareholders may be evidence of that company's financing and control (an evidential value); but they may also be a source of information on the financial activities of certain individuals (an informational value). Many records of informational value are case papers of some kind. Among the records of a social service department, the evidential values will reside in the records of policy-making, and the statistical effect of the service. The informational

71

values may well prove to be in the case files which document the individuals affected by the service. These are likely to be voluminous, and difficult to manage.[10]

Informational values have had unfavourable comment from archival writers. The Grigg report accepted the principle that no record should be preserved simply because it might be valuable either for historical or for genealogical research.[11] This view follows naturally from the report's decision to give primacy to administrative values. There is a corollary, however. If an ephemeral record is destroyed after appraisal, the judgement of the appraiser is not necessarily to be called in question if, thereafter, someone happens to call for that record. All records carry *some* information, and if it is granted that most records (in terms of bulk) must be destroyed, and only a small proportion of the most valuable preserved, then we must reconcile ourselves to losing items which some people would have liked to keep. Nevertheless, it would be perverse to carry the principle further, and say that because there is likely to be public interest in a record, that is a contraindication to adjudging it worthy of retention. The public pays, ultimately, and so has a basic right to have access, and to have its wishes respected in appraisal.

The concept of permanence

There are some archives which are national treasures and which we must seriously strive to keep for ever. There are not many of these: each reader will doubtless have his own list. Since archives are inherently bulky, some of these treasures will occupy a lot of space. One person might accept the great series of medieval rolls held in the PRO as being in this category; but another might include only Domesday Book and Magna Carta. There are two characteristics of archives in this category of permanence, which serve to define it: they are 'worth a visit' (in the words of the guidebooks) by the public; and they have been or are the subject of intensive study and publication by scholars. For these, the best form of descriptive finding aid is the full transcript. To preserve them for ever (setting aside doubts about the overweening nature of human pride and self-absorption) requires costly and elaborate preparations: in fact, it would require precautions which not many countries have been prepared to undertake, such as bomb-proof storage dug into mountain rock.[12]

Archives, nevertheless, are voluminous. Every year the PRO takes in records which will fill an additional mile of shelving, and this after rigorous selection. It is clear that there must be two main retention categories, which might be labelled as follows:

(i)   'these I am going to try to keep for ever'
(ii) 'these I am going to keep as long as they last, with reasonable care'

The second category might be termed, in more official language, as destined for indefinite retention. The length of time meant by the indefinite may, sometimes, be extended by using microfilm or other copying systems. Good quality storage, a controlled environment and careful access management are still required; but there is a notional acceptance of the view (probably not explicitly stated anywhere) that there is a limit to the resources which are to be committed to the conservation of these materials.

A good way to calculate where this limit may be is by working out the financial implications. In most circumstances it should be possible to establish what is the cost of keeping a given quantity of archives over a given period of time. Capital expenditure amortised, plus recurrent costs (including staffing), can be divided by the number of linear metres of shelving in use. This will provide the cost per year of each linear metre. In the case of the most valuable materials, the usefulness of this information is limited, since if the archival material has unquestionably passed the tests of permanent retention, then it is not justifiable to introduce economies which would have the effect of directly reducing its life expectancy. In all other cases, it is a piece of information that should be known and published. Cost is one of the two specific and measurable criteria to be taken into account in the course of appraisal. The second measurable criterion is, of course, the actual rate of reference access to the class over its period of existence. It is hard to see how any sort of systematic appraisal can be carried out without these two pieces of information. With them, a cost—value ratio can be established, which will be the basis of a retention decision.

Cost—value calculations are not the whole answer to appraisal problems, but they are a necessary part of the data on which appraisal decisions may be based. A document's value to research, and the value of the research itself, are both matters of opinion; though of course it should be an informed opinion, held by someone with experience of research. The judgement eventually reached should be one which has a term of years in mind. Thus records which have successfully passed the archival appraisal test, will have done so as 'to be archived and kept 100 years'; or 'indefinitely' (i.e. in category (ii) above); very rarely, or perhaps even never (nowadays) 'to be kept for ever'. We live in a world of relative values, and in one in which values have to be quantified.

Sampling

The main advance in appraisal theory has occurred in connection with the sampling of long series. An important RAMP study by Felix Hull has clarified issues which had long been doubtful.[13] This report comments that the appraisal process itself, being concerned with the selection of some material and the rejection of others, is itself a form of sampling. In this sense the debate and use of archival sampling will continue indefinitely into the future. Apart from this, the Hull report may have come almost too late. We have already begun to think about using computers to interpret archival data, and about the special problems of appraising data bases held in machine-readable form. These two developments may mean that the experience painfully learned about how to sample hard copy records may not continue to be useful long into the future.

The Hull report makes it clear that there are several preconditions before sampling can validly be used as a solution to appraisal problems. These are specified in the *Guidelines for sampling procedures* which it contains. In particular the technique can only be applied where there is a series of uniform or homogeneous records which cannot be retained in the original or in a microform copy.

Four alternative methods of sampling are discussed:

1. Keeping typical examples.   This traditional method of indicating the presence and general nature of a class which has been destroyed is still sometimes useful. Finding aids should indicate what has been kept and why. The technique is perhaps particularly apt in a museum context, since the items retained are mainly useful for illustration or display.

2. Purposive sampling.   This too has been a traditional method used by archivists dealing with large classes,

especially where these have not been fully homogeneous. The principle is to keep those items which relate to a selected subject (for example, all records relating to riot), or to defined individuals (for example, all records mentioning persons included in *Who's Who*).

3. Systematic sampling.   In this case a rule is adopted for the selection of certain items. Topographical examples may be taken where there are topographical items within the series. An alphabetical criterion can be used if the items are alphabetically coded or titled. Numerical or serial sampling can be used if they are numbered; and chronological sampling if the records are kept by date. The selection rule will specify which are to be kept: one from each topographical point, all representatives of the letters H-P, every 25th numerical entry; records for every year ending in '5'. These examples do not suggest the best possibilities which this method has. A systematic sample could be devised to record and illustrate specially characteristic items of information, and may be based upon significant patterns or periodicities in the records.

4. Random sampling.   This is the only method which allows a scientifically satisfactory evaluation of the quantitative meaning of the whole class, calculated from the surviving sample. In a true random sample, each item has in principle an exactly equal chance of being chosen to represent the series. There must be a numerical method of identifying items, and a random number table, or its equivalent, must be used. The size of the sample taken is also significant.

5. Mixed systems.   The discussion of the problem in the Hull report and elsewhere suggests that in an archival context no single one of these sampling methods is likely to be entirely satisfactory. A mixture of methods is possible, provided that they are applied in an order which does not interfere with the operation of the system. Thus it is possible to combine random and purposive samples, but the random sample must be applied first, and any resulting empty spaces in the second sample would have to be supplied with cross references.

Prediction of research values

The most difficult part of archival appraisal is the prediction of future research value. It is notorious that research themes, and the sources for them, were neglected in the past, and that new lines of research come about as a result of the initiatives or discoveries of gifted individuals. Yet at the same time, appraisal is necessarily based upon the prediction of likely lines of development in research.

Prediction can never be wholly successful. Nevertheless, systematic attempts to marshal the existing evidence both on the nature of the sources and the research which has been done on them will lead the appraiser a good way towards success. It is also possible to stimulate new research by publicising sources. These two activities were undertaken in a series of major conferences organised by NARS in the early 1970s, the results of which were published by the Ohio University Press.[14]

Another way in which the course of research can be predicted to some extent is by encouraging archivists to maintain an active role in research fields. The archives service may set itself the goal of being an active research institute, and many do so. It is doubtless easier for a specialist archives service to achieve this position than a generalist one. The Glasgow University Archives, which has an important special interest in shipping archives, is known as a centre of information in that subject and several publications have been the result.[15] On the other hand, a county record office, which contains multifarious archives from all sorts of sources, but whose area of specialisation is territorial, may find that though it has successfully become a centre of local studies, its best chance of achieving prominence as a research institute is by developing a specific interest proper to the area. The Clwyd Record Office, for instance, has developed an expertise in the history of mining.[16] Archivists must remain active participants in subjects of research on which their office has significant holdings, or else they will not be able to represent research interests in administrative settings.[17]

Conclusion

The discussion so far has suggested that appraisal is something which may occur once and for all at a given moment. Though this does happen, it is not the best way.

Firstly, there may be retrospective appraisal. A recent American commentator has suggested that appraisal decisions made too loosely in the past should be reconsidered.[18] Of course, this only applies to affirmative appraisal decisions, for the sad fact is that records which are turned down at appraisal are usually destroyed. Should we go back over our archival holdings, test them against the frequency of research reference, and reappraise? Most archivists would agree that there are cases where this might be beneficial, but also perhaps that the dangers outweigh the possible benefits. Academic fashions exist just as much as clothing fashions. If the passing of one fashion and the coming of another were to lead to the wholesale destruction of archives, we would ultimately be sorry.

Secondly, appraisal is a process rather than an event. The current American basic manual says

> Records appraisal is best considered as a *process* that requires extensive staff preparation, a thorough analysis of the origin and characteristics of record series, a knowledge of techniques for the segregation and selection of records, an awareness of the development of research methodologies and needs, and a sequential consideration of administrative, research and archival values.[19]

Delegation

Even where the conservational aims are redefined narrowly, archives management and storage is expensive. It may be necessary to call in help, particularly where a large accumulation of archives, bearing on some definable subject area, is concerned. Storage and access costs could often be borne by an appropriate research institution, at the cost of taking that material away from the archives repository which in strict custom should have looked after them. Institutional pride may be hurt, but it is the overall increase of resources which is the end benefit to society. Thus the PRO's decision to allow the University of Newfoundland to retain the residue of the Crew Lists may be applauded because it brought into play new repository space and new staffing resources.[20]

Many appraisal decisions may be aided by introducing the possibility of delegation to a specialist agency. In many countries it has been established that any sort of archival materials may be deposited in publicly financed repositories, without cost to the owner, and without loss of ownership. Of course, in this case, the burden of appraisal decisions is shifted to the repository's staff, who will approach the problem in the light of their own stated aims.

The Process of Accessioning

Since provenance and custodial history remain important in interpreting archival sources, it is essential that consignments of archives should be registered on arrival, and that the register of accessions remains as a permanent record. This requirement is one of the points of difference between libraries and archives services.

The accessions register may be used for two purposes other than the recording of the archive's arrival and origin. These are:

(a) to provide some sort of acknowledgement to the originator or former custodian of the archive;

(b) to control the various processes in the archives service.

It has been suggested therefore that the best form of accessions register might be a loose-leaf one, in which each accession is described on a triplicated form. The top copy, which should be treated as permanent, would contain details of the archive, its origin, provenance and custodial history, including the date of transfer. The second copy might carry a printed letter of acknowledgement, with the archive service's address, which could be sent to the transferor of the archive. The third copy, to be kept perhaps in the central workroom, might contain columns for completion when the various stages were complete: sorting, boxing, shelving, listing, indexing, repair.[21]

Since central registration of archival transfers is a national interest, a note might be appropriate for sending to the NRA. This might be done by means of a fourth copy.

The registration of new accessions therefore begins the administrative control of the material, as it passes through the processing stage towards the stage of final exploitation.

Archival arrangement

The arrangement of archives is an essential operation in the process of managing the information contained in them. Arrangement is also an important step in the conservation of the materials, governing their disposition and housing in the repository. For the same reason, it is a process essential to their administrative control. But in addition, arrangement is an essential part of the eventual exploitation of the archive in reference and research: it is an aspect of intellectual as well as administrative control. The arrangement of an archive is an essential part of the process which will lead to the creation of a representation file, the basis of a system of finding aids, which will provide the user (including staff users) with both a conceptual and an administrative overview of the material. Most importantly, however, the arrangement of an assembly of archives perpetuates and demonstrates relationships between its components, explaining and authenticating the significance of the information in them. The activities which support this have traditionally been known as the moral defence of archives, and are central to the professional ethic of archivists.[1]

The Moral Defence of Archives

T.R. Schellenberg observed that arrangement

> is largely a process of grouping individual documents into meaningful units and of grouping such units in a meaningful relation to one another. An archivist, continually and instinctively, must bring order and relation to unrelated things by sorting and categorising − to the end of revealing the content and significance of the records with which he works.[2]

Initially, the main purpose of archival arrangement is to reduce disorder and restore (or introduce) order into the mass of materials which makes up an archival group or collection. This is a management exercise, not merely a physical process: it involves research and planning, and it ought to be carried out at a level which will provide overall control over what are usually large quantities of material. The aim is to organise these quantities into manageable divisions and subdivisions, but also to protect and demonstrate the meaning, authority and significance of the information content. Moral defence is concerned with managing information, even though it may depend on an examination and ordering of physical materials to do so.

The aim of moral defence is to establish the evidential significance of the archives. Why should this be necessary? In a library or documentation centre, any particular bibliographic item should be able to explain itself. Its title identifies it, and its content can be adequately delineated by an abstract. By contrast, an archival accumulation has to have additional information which can explain to the user the basic facts about the system and organisation which created the material originally. Single documents or sets of documents taken from an archive are usually not fully self-explanatory. They are most often known by a reference code rather than by a title, and neither the meaning nor the authenticity of such fragments can be taken without investigation.

The work of an archivist in arrangement therefore begins with the study of the provenance of the material being processed, and of the system which was employed to bring it into existence, and to store and use it during its period of currency; it is also often necessary to understand the custodial history of the material since that initial period. By placing the archives in an order which is the same as, or which corresponds to, or reflects, that of the original system, an archivist is providing a statement on meaning and authenticity: this statement is the main strongpoint of the moral defence of the archives, for it ensures that the evidential meaning of the archives will be understood for ever afterwards. To do this work, archivists must spend time in research, investigating and analysing the provenance of their material, the administrative systems which, historically, have produced the archive, and the story of its adventures since.

T.R. Schellenberg said:

> Basic to practically all activities of the archivist is his analysis of records. This analysis involves him in studies of the organisational and functional origins of records to obtain information on their provenance, subject, content and interrelations . . . Analytical activities are the essence of an archivist's work; the other activities

that are based on them are largely of a physical nature.[3]

The term 'evidential' is used because (as has often been pointed out), archives have the special characteristic that, since they actually formed part of the administrative or business process which their information relates to, what they say carries a particular weight as primary evidence for statements made, or conclusions drawn, about that process.

It is therefore clear that archival arrangement cannot generally use universal classifications, since the material cannot be sorted into predetermined categories. The categories (subgroups) which can be used are discovered by carrying out an analysis of the origins and functions of the archive-creating agency, and then by a study of the relationships between physically or organisationally associated sets (classes or series).

Since an important objective is the administrative control of the material, groups, subgroups and classes of archives must in the end be of manageable size and shape. Archival management must take account of this need. Nevertheless, the principal purpose of archival arrangement must be the moral defence of the archive, and its outcome should in general be the sorting of the materials into an order, and into groupings, which demonstrate their original meaning.

The chief source of information used by archivists in their research into the provenance, archival order and custodial history of the group is the materials themselves. By noting their physical shape, reference codes or other control information in them, the names and status of officials or important personalities mentioned, and the functions of each as reflected in the documents, the analyst can establish the outlines of an administrative history for the group. Additional sources of information will frequently have to be found, in reference books, secondary works, or sometimes even in the recollections of people associated with the creating organisation.

Some groups or collections do not have a clearly perceived provenance, or an easily outlined administrative or custodial history. These may have to be treated in ways which seem (at least) to set aside the rule of restoring original order. The arrangement of materials in this special case is discussed separately.

Levels of Arrangement

Following these principles of moral defence, the archivist's first action in taking over a newly acquired mass of archival material is to decide how to break it down into a structured series of levels and groupings. Since they are based upon an analysis of the originating system, these breakdowns both assist a logical understanding of the makeup of the archive accumulation, but also perpetuate and reinforce the original relationships of parts of the archive to each other.[4]

The number and nature of the levels used to control a group depend not only on its original structure but on the overall management needs of the archives service itself. It is important that the archivist should be quite clear how many levels are to be used, which level is being treated at any particular moment, and how the different levels relate to each other. The relationship of levels within groups should be understood not only within the group being treated but also between the groups in the repository's holdings and even perhaps across those in the holdings of several repositories. Finding aids might include a statement on the levels used, and this could appear at the beginning, or in the introduction.

The most commonly used levels of arrangement are called groups, subgroups, classes and items. For the sake of clarity, these terms should be used. But if there are more than four levels (in a more complex arrangement), it is probably better to use numbers, rather than terms such as sub-subgroup. This is illustrated in the table on p. 84, which explains the numeration used.

The division of an archive into levels is always a most important part of its arrangement. There will always be at least two, and probably at least four, levels in any particular accumulation of archives. Each level needs to be dealt with in an appropriate way. The higher levels, in which larger groupings are dealt with more or less in bulk, can be considered as 'macro' levels; the lower ones, where documents or other units can be taken item by item, and in detail, are 'micro' levels. The concepts of macro and micro levels relate principally to archival description, but since arrangement and description are closely interlinked activities in archival management, a full definition of the levels normally perceptible can be given here.

This analysis of levels in archival arrangement, and the

names they should be given, is based on recent writing, mainly American, but there has been discussion for many years, and in many countries.

Sir Hilary Jenkinson established the definition of an *Archive Group* in his Manual of 1922.[5] He naturally based his thought upon the practice and terminology of the PRO, which used the ministries or government departments as the basis of its principal divisions of material. The archives emanating from each of these was known as an Archive Group. Within these the PRO used the class as its only subdivision and main control point. Within classes, individual items ('pieces' in PRO terminology) were listed serially.

In practice a careful study of PRO descriptions shows that levels intermediate to these were at times admitted, but usually were not reflected in the reference codes. Both then and now reference codes in the PRO consist simply of a letter-number reference which suggests only three levels: for example, FO 84/2030 refers to file no.2030 within class 84 of the Foreign Office archive group. In citation, a fourth level often appears when individual papers upon the file are quoted. The example would then be FO84/2030, no.140, which is a letter from Lord Salisbury to Sir Edward Malet written in May 1890.

North American practice, both in public archives services and in manuscript libraries, was based upon a variation of the same principle. The American 'record group' could either be the same as the British archive group (i.e. the archives emanating from a particular autonomous administrative unit), or it could be a portmanteau within which were assembled, for administrative convenience, the archives of a number of originating units. These units might be linked in this way because they had some common characteristic, but also might be brought together arbitrarily.[6]

There was no development of theory from this point in Britain, but by the early 1960s, O.W. Holmes, in a staff instruction paper for NARS, proposed a standard five-level system.[7] Simultaneously, faced with growing administrative instability at archive group level, P.J. Scott, writing from his Australian experience, suggested in 1966 the possibility of abandoning the archive group as the main administrative control, and adopting the series (class) as an alternative.[8] Work on the development of the automated system for archival description, SPINDEX, further habituated American archivists to working at multiple, but clearly distinguished, levels. SPINDEX incorporates numerical codes which identify the level, and can provide up to eight.[9] However it was not until the publication of the work of two American analysts, R.H. Lytle and R. Berner, that the distinctions underlying the principle of archival levels became fully clear.[10] Lack of precision in the meaning of the terms had certainly fogged the issues to a considerable extent up till then. In particular, there had been widespread confusion as to the distinction between subgroups and classes; this can have serious consequences as classes are frequently designated as the principal level of control in an archives service.

The definitions used in this book and in MAD are based upon the work of Richard H. Lytle, in the light of comments made by R. Berner, but have also been modified to take account of British practice.

In the table below, a model showing a system of nine levels of archival arrangement is shown:

0.	Repository level	Management levels
1.	Archive group	
2.	Group/collection	
3.	Subgroup	Macro Description levels
4.	Possible sub-subgroups	
5.	Class	Main control level
6.	Possible subclasses	
7.	Item	Micro Description levels
8.	Piece	

Source: *Manual of Archival Description*, 1984

Level 0: the repository

This level is apparent only where multi-repository sets of archives are concerned. It is clear that archives are distributed among repositories, and therefore this must logically be regarded as the upper level of arrangement. The level is numbered zero, since it will not be used in arrangements of material within the repository. It will be important, though, when a national or regional catalogue is published.[11]

The reference code of an archive cited in a research document must carry as its first element an identification of the repository where it is kept.

Level 1: archive group

The practice is widespread of gathering the holdings of a repository into large categories with some common characteristic related to provenance. When used in this way (like an American record group), this level of arrangement is operative only in the organisation of the repository and in its published finding aids, and not essentially in any physical arrangement of the material. Repositories can certainly be found where components of the main archive groups are stored together in dedicated strongrooms, but it will be broadly recognised that there is a strong element of management convenience in this system of allocating space.

The purpose of level 1 is to help with the orderly administration of the repository, the application of legal provisions governing certain types of archive, and sometimes with the production of co-operative finding aids. A logical analysis of the holdings of a repository, in which the material is divided into archive groups, is also a help to users. The division of the holdings into archive groups may also help to allocate responsibilities to members of staff.

Archive groups (in the present use of the term) are known in the PRO as the basis of the distinction between the contents of the different volumes of the *Guide*. When the PRO's new building at Kew was opened, this distinction was used as the basis for the decision to remove some of the holdings to the new building, and retain some in the old.[12] This illustrates that there is an important principle of archival arrangement present, even though it may remain a notional (and not essentially a physical) aspect of archival management.

In local record offices, the archive groups are usually based on broad areas of provenance. The minimum number of archive groups is usually three: official, ecclesiastical and private. Increasingly, a larger number of archive groups is being established. A typical list is given in the discussion on classification. Archive groups may also be distinguished between accumulations of archives which are, and which are not, subject to the public records acts.

In specialist repositories there is no established practice, but there is a tendency to introduce archive groups to distinguish between materials of internal and external provenance, where this is relevant.

Level 2: group

The group is the largest unit of management related to physical control. Since a group usually comprises a relatively large amount of material, it should be defined in a way which will bring together the whole of a major *fonds*, or single complex source of archival material. What is intended is a 'natural' division, something which arises from the nature of the archive-creating agency whose products are being administered.

Outside the PRO, the normal term for what is here called the group, is 'collection'. Originating in librarianship, the term has come to be used loosely for any set of archival materials which arises from a common source, as well as for accumulations which have been assembled artificially. It would be preferable if 'group' could be used where the materials are a natural archival accumulation, but where collections consist of materials wholly or partly unrelated archivally, brought together by a collector, these may also, at least in many cases, be treated as groups.

For the sake of clarity, it should be recalled that a group as defined here resembles what Jenkinson called an archive group. His classic definition, still valid in the PRO, may be repeated:

> all the Archives resulting from the work of an Administration which was an organic whole, complete in itself, capable of dealing independently, without any added or external authority, with every side of any business which could normally be presented to it.[13]

This definition applies naturally, not only to the archives of government departments (for which it was originally devised) but also to such entities as business firms, the papers of eminent individuals, landed estates, churches, university departments, and to most organisations which are structured into more than one sub-unit.

Level 3: subgroup

Groups may be (and usually are) subdivided naturally. Subgroups may be formed which correspond either to

(a) administrative subdivisions in the originating organisation, or

(b) functional groupings in the material itself.

The first case is the easier to deal with. If the group consists of the archives of a business firm, for example, then the subgroups will consist of those which derive from each of the firm's departments — company secretary, legal adviser, public relations office, etc. These will be 'natural' divisions, distinguishable by the original markings on the archives themselves, or by an analysis of the company's departmental structure.

The second case may be more difficult, but may be necessary in cases where the originating agency had no clear structural divisions. The success of this approach depends on the archivist's ability to analyse the functions distinguishable in his material. The papers of a private individual, for example, often cannot be arranged according to the organisational structures of that individual's original system, for he probably did not have one. In this case, functional subgroups may be established by grouping together the papers arising from an appointment to a particular post, membership of a particular movement, participation in a particular project or campaign, dealing with a particular activity, or corresponding with a particular individual. These are arbitrary divisions, though they may correspond with an embryonic classification which may have been in the mind of the originator, but not formally expressed.

It is important to distinguish subgroups from classes. Subgroups represent *organisational* or structural divisions of the originating agency of the group. The distinction is not based upon any *physical* likeness or relationship the records may have: this is the province of the class.

87

Level 4

Additional levels are needed to allow for sub-subgroups. It is quite likely that a group will have several levels of subdivision based upon structural relationships in the original system. If the group is a business firm, and subgroups its departments, then each subgroup will be subdivided so that the sections, offices and subordinate management units can be distinguished. If the group is a political party, subgroups may be based upon the constituency parties, and below this, on borough, ward and trade association parties which occupy constitutional positions in the structure. There can be any number of subordinate levels below the subgroup, and where this is so, it may be best to abandon the standard labels (group, subgroup, etc) and use numerals. A number is preferable to the ugly term 'sub-subgroup', and if there are more levels to be inserted, the lack of suitable plain language terminology becomes more acute.

Level 5: class

'Class' is a British term for what is known internationally as 'series'. A class is the basic unit of administrative control of archives, and hence of arrangement. It is a division based primarily upon physical characteristics in the records, but these arise from the administrative systems of the originating organisation.

A standard definition is that of P.J. Scott:

> a group of record items which, being controlled by numbers or other symbols, are in the same sequence of numbers or symbols, or which, being uncontrolled by numbers or symbols, result from the same accumulation or filing process and are of similar physical shape and informational content.[14]

This definition seems rather abstract. This is because it has to cover an enormous variety of different cases. In actual practice, it is usually fairly easy to recognise a class of records because of its unitary character. A simple alternative definition might concentrate on this, and emphasise that a class is an organised assembly of archives or records which belong together in a system and which have a common name.

Classes, like any of the other levels of arrangement, may be of any size. Some are very large: the central filing unit in an

88

administrative department, for example. This may contain many thousands of items, papers or folders. It may occupy a large number of filing cabinets or vertical file units, it may spread over several rooms. There may be a heavy turnover of papers coming in and going out of it. There may be an extension to it in the intermediate store. If the mass belongs together, is run as a common system, has broadly a common physical appearance, and is called by a common name ('the central filing system') then it is clearly a class, and can be used as a unit of management.

Alternatively, classes can be small. A register of particular occurrences, for instance, could be a class, and might consist of only one item — say a bound volume containing the registration details. Accruals of new data may be either rare or constant — frequency of reference is not important in the definition.

If classes are to be the unit of management, it makes sense to treat them as units when archives are being arranged. As they are distinguished essentially by physical characteristics, it should be natural to store them together. Allowance may have to be made for the accrual of new material to an existing class.

Level 6: subclasses

Classes may have to be subdivided where there was an original subordinate or dependent system. For example, a set of files within a filing system may have been divided out and given a subset of reference numbers. The new subordinate system may subsequently be the basis of a separate class, or may have been reabsorbed into the original one. Either way, it may best be treated as a subclass.

Level 7: item

Items too are physical units, but they are also units of management. An item is the lowest physically convenient unit of archival material: a folder, volume, bundle or box. It is a physical entity, but not necessarily an indivisible one. It should be possible to give items a unique reference code or title by which they can be recognised; and it should be possible to pick the item up as a unit.

Items may be arranged in relation to each other. The final order should be one which reflects the original system by which they were created. Physically, items may be conserved by any convenient means, by boxing them in tens, for instance; but a record of the original provenance should be kept, and should be expressed in the archival reference codes written on the outside of the box, and in structural descriptions.

Each item may contain a number of pieces — letters in a file of correspondence, for instance, or pages in a volume. Since these are not units of management, it should not usually be necessary to arrange these lower units, Where component pieces are in confusion, and had an original arrangement, this can be restored. Otherwise they could be sorted chronologically or alphabetically within the folder. Many archives services would avoid putting too much effort into arrangement at this level. The essential thing is to arrange the items within their classes, and control the classes as units of management.

Classification

Levels of arrangement can be expressed logically by means of a classification scheme. The PRO does not have such a scheme, and since it officially uses only three levels, has not found one necessary as an explanation of its system of arrangement. In other archives services, the attraction of classifications has always been felt, and a great deal of effort has been put into devising them, in many cases under the influence of library practice.

Experiment in some library-based archives services has shown that, generally, universal subject classifications are not suitable for determining the arrangement of archives. More useful schemes are based upon an analysis of functions and/or of record types. Clearly, the guiding principles of an archival classification scheme should be the same as those for archival arrangement. The scheme may however incorporate some additional elements, such as provision for some degree of subject retrieval.

Historically, classification schemes for local record offices began where a particular kind of archive accumulation was found to be held by more than one repository. County record offices usually hold the ancient archives of their county, the archives of the Courts of Quarter Sessions. They found themselves faced with the problem of arranging these at an early stage in their development. In one sense, these archives are unique in each case: the personnel who created them in each county were different individuals, they dealt with different cases, and frequently the system they devised to discharge their responsibilities had some unique feature. However, at the same time, the various courts of quarter sessions were generically similar, subject to the same ruling statutes and government intervention, and produced similar types of archive. Consequently the county record offices which first began to arrange and describe their quarter sessions archives established an arrangement which could be copied in other counties. As a result, the Essex/Bedford scheme for quarter sessions has become a system used (with some local modifications) by all other counties. It is a flexible scheme, based upon a combination of function and form.[15]

Similar circumstances led to the wide adoption of a small number of classification schemes in the case of other archive series. The main ones deal with the archives of parishes, Poor Law authorities, modern county councils, churches, and educational administration.

Many archives services have also developed general classification schemes which govern their entire holdings. These have not been copied or become in any sense standard, except in the sense that the procedure is familiar. Outside the PRO, archivists have not dissented from the view that library examples were to be followed as far as possible. As will be seen from the example given below, the principle on which overall schemes are constructed is similar to that of the quarter sessions scheme: function modified by form.

One of the advantages of a classification scheme is that it can provide a system of reference codes which reflect the relationships between the components of an archive. Although there has been no uniformity of practice, in what follows an attempt has been made to establish some standard conventions. One of these is that levels 1—4 should be represented by alphabetic codes, level 5 and below by numerical ones. This convention, which is fairly widely observed, has proved useful in structuring archival descriptions in finding aid systems, and users have grown accustomed to it.

The function of a classification scheme is to formalise the archival order established during the process of arrangement, and relate it to administrative control instruments (such as location indexes) and to the finding aids generally. It can also help to introduce a degree of compatibility between the finding aids of different archives services, where these services hold groups of similar general character.

A survey of some of the main classification schemes in use in British archives services may help to illustrate these points.

An example of an overall classification is the scheme for Cheshire Record Office (slightly amended), which uses five levels:

Level 1 is represented by a single letter code:

C   County council
D   Deposited archives (from private sources)
E   Ecclesiastical archives
L   Local and statutory authorities within the county
M   Lieutenancy (militia)
N   Public records of local provenance
P   Parishes
Q   Quarter sessions
S   Schools
W   Probate archives (wills).

In the context of this record office, these divisions represent the archive groups. In this case, there are ten.

Level 2 is marked by the addition of a second alphabetical character. These are groups (only a selection is given as examples):

CE   County council: education department
EB   Ecclesiastical: Baptist churches
LB   Local authorities: borough councils
NH   Public Records: hospitals.

Level 3 is provided for particular cases. These are subgroups: only examples are shown:

EDC   Ecclesiastical: Diocese of Chester: consistory court
LBA   Local authorities: borough councils: Altrincham
NPR   Public Records: public utilities: railways.

The next level is represented by a numerical character, and refers to classes. Note that in the two examples following, level 3 is left empty.

CF 1   County council: fire brigade: research reports.

Subclasses are possible:

CH 1/1   County council: highways dept: traffic regulation orders: speed limits.

Note that an entry at the first two levels is obligatory, but below this fields may be left empty, or levels unused.

It is generally agreed that the changes in the structure of local government as a consequence of the Local Government Act 1972 should be reflected in the archival classification. Even where there was no substantial boundary change, the council that assumed power in 1974 was a new foundation, and not a modified continuation of the one set up in 1888. Even apart from this, there were usually radical changes of departmental and committee structures which would have necessitated new features in the classification. A model is therefore needed for 'new' councils. Although several record offices produced suitable schemes for their own use, there has been no observable tendency for any of them to be adopted elsewhere. An example is the scheme upon which the Kent Archives Office based its guide in 1974.[16] A model for authorities which were set up entirely new in that year, with no historical predecessors is also needed, as is one for specialised bodies.

Since parish archives exist in great numbers, several attempts have been made to establish a scheme for these. A family likeness can be seen in many of them, and the following attempts to give a fairly typical version, with modifications.[17]

Group: the individual parish

Subgroups

Incumbent	Ecclesiastical
Churchwardens	
Vestry	
Parochial Church Council	
Constables	Civil officials
Overseers of the Poor	
Surveyors of the Highways	
Parish Council or Meeting	Civil assemblies
Burial Board	
Special committees	
Charities	Other functions
Schools	
Statutory deposits (tithe)	

Sub-subgroups
  Incumbent: registration
                   glebe
                   tithe
  Churchwardens: rating
                   accounting
                   fabric/property administration, etc.

Classes
  Overseers: settlement: indemnity bonds and certificates
                          removal orders
                          examinations,
                          etc.

All local government record offices and many other archives services solicit and accept deposits of archives of external origin. Many have classification schemes which cover private, family and estate papers, and some have attempted classification work in other areas, such as the archives of industrial and business firms, and political bodies.

Archives of private origin are often regarded as one of the main archive groups. Since by tradition these are mostly deposited archives, it is common (although not universal) to designate them with the symbol 'D', and each group or collection with this designation will have additional characters to identify it as a second-level entity. In the past these characters have often been adopted on a mnemonic basis, for example

DBC   Archives of Messrs Birch, Cullimore and Co.
DDX   Miscellaneous small deposits.[18]

As the number of such deposits has grown, mnemonic characters have tended to run out. Their value in any case is limited. Probably it is best nowadays to adopt arbitrary alphabetic symbols from the start, as DAA, DAB, etc. In this way the distinction between subgroups (whose reference code is alphabetic) and classes (numerical codes) can be maintained. If this convention is disregarded, then groups can be given serial numbers for identification purposes: D103, etc., and this would have the advantage that group reference codes could be made the same as the accession reference.

The portmanteau group represented in the example by DDX, is widely agreed to be a useful catch-all for deposits which consist of single documents or small numbers of unrelated individual items. It demonstrates, at a lower level, the administrative convenience of the American record

94

group.

There is as yet no classification based upon the archives of manufacturing or business firms. L. McDonald has done the basic analytical work but has not yet published a scheme.[19] It is clear that the general outline will follow an analysis of the company's structure and functions, in the usual way:

Source of authority	Archive-creating structure
Governing body	Shareholders' meetings
Membership	Registers, transfers
Legal instrument	Charter, etc.
Controlling body	Board of directors
Committees	Executive, finance, etc.
Officials, departments	Chairman, managing director departmental heads
Finance	Accounting depts etc.
Legal	Statutory, patents, etc.
Process	Manufacturing controls

It will be noticed that in the absence of an existing classification which has been made up by an examination of actual archive accumulations, a structure can be made up by analysing either the actual organisation and functions of a specific company, or, less satisfactorily, doing the analysis in the abstract, from first principles and a knowledge of how companies are structured.

The theoretical analysis of a company given in the table above is a functional and not a subject classification. The terms in the left-hand column, which are based upon a theoretical analysis of a company's make-up, do not correspond to the headings (some of them broadly similar) which could appear in a subject classification. One record office uses a broad division of business archives into three sub-groups (Administration, Finance, Operational); but this is based upon a simple subject classification and is in many cases operable only by allocating particular archive entities to one of the categories, irrespective of its actual place in an archival context. A financial record, for instance a ledger, may be produced and kept by a production department in a manufacturing firm: in an archival analysis these volumes ought to be placed with the records of the appropriate department, not transferred to those of the finance office. Adopting a subject classification always means that some must be allocated to a category out of context; whereas a functional classification will provide a correct archival category for each component.

The West Sussex Record Office has devised a classification scheme for political archives which is based upon a simple matrix.[20]

Level 1: Political records

Level 2:

Party		Constituency	
LA	Labour	AR	Arundel
CO	Conservative	CH	Chichester
LI	Liberal	CR	Crawley
SD	Social Democrat	HO	Horsham
CM	Communist	MS	Mid-Sussex
NF	National Front	SH	Shoreham
EC	Ecology	WO	Worthing
		EU	European constituency.

To incorporate the double classification at the second level, archival entities must be given a double reference code, e.g. LA/CH. Logically, however, the constituency entries are on a level below that of the party entries, and so must appear second in the code. Subordinate entities within the parties (constituency, area, ward, etc.) can then be numbered or coded as Level 3 (subgroups), but, since they are subdivisions of the parties (and not of the constituencies) the code for these must appear before the constituency code: e.g. LA/3CH — Labour Party, constituency party, Midhurst.

Standard classes

Several schemes recognise that classes often exist within subgroups on a regularly repeating pattern. Thus a subgroup which contains a committee, will normally have classes for agenda papers, minutes, reports and submissions, and correspondence. In some cases it is possible to establish a standard pattern in which regularly repeating classes are given the same numerical code; when a class abnormally is not represented, the field represented by the code would then be left empty. The Modern Records Centre at Warwick University has such a scheme, operated as far as possible over the entire holdings:[21]

/1   Minutes, agendas, reports
/2   Financial records
/3   Correspondence files
/4   Publications of the creating organisation
/5   Other publications
/6   Subclasses (e.g. personal papers of an individual official kept together)
/7   Miscellaneous
/8   Diaries
/9   Agreements
/10 Press cuttings
/11 Reports
/12 Photographs
/13 Statistics

Item and subclass references are given after the regularly repeating class references: e.g.

MSS.5/1/4
    Collection reference (accession no.5)
      Class reference (minutes)
        Item reference (vol.4)

The purpose of this repeating pattern is to help users identify relevant material across a number of rather similar small deposits. Provision has to be made for the arrangement and referencing of collections which do not fit the pattern.

Alternative methods of arrangement

The methods of arrangement discussed so far are all natural rather than artificial. They are based on the principle of provenance and of original order. The archivist establishes a logical structure based upon the original system. This is equally true with arrangement and classification at macro or at micro levels, at archive group, group or class, or item level.

Cases where there was no original system or where analysis of the original system does not give useful results, are not common, but they do exist. Where they are encountered, archivists may have to apply an artificial method.

There are four possible principles of operation, listed in order of theoretical preference: function, form, alphabetical-chronological, and subject.

Analysis by function is often little different from an analysis of actual functional structures in the originating organisation, and so has already been discussed. Equally, it was noted that form (the physical character or format of the archival material) has often been used as a modifying element in archival classifications. Form is usually more suitable for identifying classes, and may not be successful if used as the principle for subgroups.

An arrangement of papers by alphabetical order of document title, applicable person, etc., or a chronological arrangement, or a combination of these, is sometimes the best way of dealing with a sequence of loose papers, especially a collection of correspondence. In fact, letters are such a common component of personal archives that there is probably a case for suggesting a standard method of procedure for them. Letters usually have six possible fields by any of which they might be sorted in particular circumstances:

1. writer
2. writer's address
3. recipient
4. recipient's address
5. date
6. subjects mentioned in the text

If the group is archival, the archivist will seek to discover how the accumulation was built up. The correspondence file of a business might be based on a system of subject filing, in which letters to the organisation, and copies of letters written by the organisation, would be kept together where they dealt with a particular theme. On the other hand, the correspondence file of a private person, though containing the same components, might always have been stored in order of the names of writers/recipients, or in order of date sent/received, without regard to subject. A pure subject sorting would be difficult to achieve in the absence of an original filing system, since individual letters can contain references to any number of subjects at the same time. An alphabetical or alpha-chronological order (in so far as it can be established) would seem to be the best way to deal with this situation, especially if the finding aids can include an index. There is no rule which can override a common-sense solution.

Reference coding

All the classification schemes illustrated use a notation which serves to link one heading to another, and to preserve the hierarchical order of levels. These notations are customarily also used as part of the reference codes which identify actual archival materials. Because of this, the allocation of a suitable reference code is an important part of archival arrangement and description. It solidifies and establishes the arrangement which has been done, and hence the moral defence of the archives. If the reference code is derived from a classification scheme, it will permanently relate the archive to its context. If there is no classification, then the reference code can still reflect the methods of arrangement used within the repository.

Archival reference codes can have a number of uses.

1. Identification of the document for retrieval.   A document is under control as soon as it (or its container) bears a code which is keyed to the finding aid system.

2. Identification of the document in citation.   This is an important feature. The more archival documents are used in research the more they are referred to in published and other secondary documents. It is important that the citations are accurate and intelligible. Since citations can occur over many years and in many different places, it is also important that archival reference codes, once allocated, should be permanent. It is perhaps worth noting that since archival materials often have no titles, and usually no author in the bibliographic sense, the reference code is often used in place of these items of bibliographical information. Identification requires that a full citation reference should include a code for the repository as well as for the document.

3. Recording the archival context of the document. The code may in favourable circumstances be used to demonstrate the way in which the materials quoted fit into the whole group, subgroup or class. This is particularly so when it has proved possible to incorporate some indication of level.

4. Security. A document bearing a repository's reference code is more difficult either to misplace or to steal.

It is not easy to combine all these objectives satisfactorily, especially in repositories which have large or complex holdings. There is an order of priority, and clearly the first of the quoted objectives must be the most fundamental. This makes it possible for some repositories to abandon objective (3) as unattainable, and simply allocate serial numbers. Most archives services however give at least the group or collection code in addition to a finding number, and thus take a step towards achieving this objective.

Archival reference codes often use mnemonic alphabetical symbols. This is a useful method as long as the supply of intelligible alphabetical codes holds out. After this, a mnemonic system becomes rather odd. Perhaps it is sound advice to avoid it from the beginning, where there is choice. The PRO's semi-mnemonic system (group codes only) has been partially abandoned because of the large number of archive groups now in the system.

Temporary reference codes are also common, especially where a newly acquired group has been given an accession number. If accession numbers are retained in use for any length of time, there is a risk that they will prevent the attainment of objective (2). It is probably better, in most cases, if the permanent reference code could be allocated at an early stage. The problem about this is that if the code is to reflect the considered arrangement of the materials, then it cannot be allocated until this work has been done. If this is a management problem in the repository, then consideration should be given to the possibility of using the accession number as the permanent identification. Systems which use a serial number identification avoid this problem.

Ideally, a final reference code should be permanently but unobtrusively written on each document, in order to achieve objective (4). In practice, this is rarely possible. The best that can usually be done is to write the code on the containers at item level. If any part of the accumulation is taken out of the repository, for use elsewhere, exhibition, or repair, the opportunity could be taken of writing on the codes.

Physical arrangement

So far the discussion has centred upon the theory of archival arrangement. The practical process, however, is known as sorting. It is customary to point out that the physical resources of an archives service should include suitable secure space for carrying it out. A workroom with benches and shelves is usually suggested as the right environment. This area should if possible be close to the conservation unit, so that damaged pieces can be repaired, and so that steps can be taken to prevent moulds or pests getting into the repository. It should also be conveniently placed for moving the materials into storage.

The physical process of sorting has priority over any other part of the activity of arrangement. It is only by sorting that the information necessary to proper arrangement can be found, and management decisions taken concerning the treatment of the group. No other method of procedure ever turns out satisfactorily. This point is insisted on because there is a tendency for inexperienced workers to try to list and store parts of the group piecemeal, to avoid preliminary sorting. This method nearly always means that the earlier sections of the work have to be done again, and that there is no effective overall management of the operation.

Archives once arranged should be boxed and stored, so that the storage location may be keyed to the reference codes, and a shelf list prepared.

Traditional practice is to store the components of an archive entity together, in structural order. This method has the great advantage that the actual physical layout of the archive preserves and demonstrates its archival relationships: storage becomes part of the moral defence of the archive. However this method may have serious disadvantages from the management viewpoint. It may demand putting big things next to small ones, and so wasting shelf space. On the other hand, it may also have management advantages. It may help when the archivists have to provide for a user who is working through a group systematically, since then the sequence of containers to be brought up corresponds to the sequence on the shelf.

It is also possible to store archives in random access order, provided, of course, that there is a finding aid which will indicate to the staff the address of each container. If this method is used (it is common in RM), then the moral defence of the archives must still be provided for, in the shape of a structural description of the archive. The original order is preserved on paper by this means. Random access storage may have considerable management benefits, in efficient use of shelf space, and in the possibility that there may be, of storing awkwardly shaped or frequently used items in handy places.[22]

A compromise between these two extremes is possible, and indeed is usual. This involves storing the bulk of a group together in structural order, but removing especially large, awkwardly shaped (such as maps) or specialised items (such as photographs) for storage in dedicated spaces. A finding aid, perhaps backed by a shelf dummy, can be used to bring these items under control.

6   Archival description

Physical control over the material is established by the arrangement of archives. To quite a considerable extent, arrangement also provides for intellectual control. Arranging the material has meant analysing it, and putting it together in a way which conserves the information so gained. Placing the materials on the shelves involves recording and demonstrating the original relationships between the components of an archival accumulation. A user who understands the original purpose of the creating organisation, and some of the most important ways in which it operated, would be able to find his way around the archives, using only its physical arrangement.[1]

Of course, this form of access assumes that users are able to examine the material physically, and also that it has been stored in something approximating to strict accordance with a structural arrangement. Neither of these requirements are easily met in practice. Documents have been boxed, and so are not easily visible; and it is not easy to write intelligible codes on the outside of the box until there has been a final listing. Awkwardly shaped items have probably been taken out of sequence and put on larger shelves. Then, there is the general question of control of access and who is to be allowed to browse among the materials in the storage area. Something more must be done to bring about a fuller intellectual control over the information recorded in the material.

To solve these problems of retrieval, access and exploitation it is necessary to write descriptions which can act as representations of the original material. These representations can then be structured and filed in different ways to make finding aids. If there are an indefinite number of representations, there can be an indefinite number of finding aids, and an indefinite number of different types of finding aid. Limitations would only be imposed by the difficulties inherent in designing representations, and by the resources needed to write them. It is clear that here, as in other sectors of information management, good initial planning is essential.

One representation file or many?

In library practice it is usual for either one or two representation files to be used. The principal one is generally the author/title catalogue, which is often backed by an additional catalogue arranged under the subject headings of a general classification scheme. Since for most purposes a representation of a book is a standard bibliographic description, catalogues can usually be compiled by duplicating these descriptions on cards, and filing the cards in different orders. In this way copies of a single representation can be used to provide a number of different representation files, and it is the varying order in which the bibliographic descriptions are arranged which makes the difference. There are only two initial requirements, which are that each description must be accurate (that is, it can genuinely serve as a representation of the original document), and that the data contained in it must be structured into fields which are appropriate as labels for sorting. These two requirements are equally necessary in archival description.

In library practice also, it is usual for one of the representation files to be arranged in approximately the same order as that of the books — generally this will be a classified (i.e. a subject) arrangement. The subject catalogue is not an exact duplication of the shelf order, because it will contain extra entries, representing books which have more than one relevant subject heading. Representations of these should appear in more than one place in the classified file. Consequently the representation file may be a better control point than the bookshelf, even where browsing is the main retrieval strategy. This principle too is applicable to archival description.

From these observations we can deduce that there ought to be a main representation file which broadly reproduces the arrangement of the original materials, but which has added entries. This main finding aid should be a structural representation file, in which the individual descriptions are put into an order which demonstrates the original system and provenance of the material, and which is based upon the structural divisions of the originating organisation. The added entries in this case will mainly be cross-references and explanatory material. However, this is radically unlike the main representation file in a library system, for such a structural finding aid cannot be used by non-expert readers unless they have learned the basic administrative history of the originating organisation.

This is why structural descriptions at group or subgroup (macro) level must normally contain at least the outline of an administrative history; and at class or item (micro) levels there must be an equivalent in the shape of an explanatory headnote. However it is necessary that normally the main representation file in an archives service should be of a structural kind, even though it has this defect, because without it the archival material will not be intelligible to users, and its contents will lose their authority as primary sources.

If the main representation file is not a good initial control point for non-expert users, then it must be backed by additional representation files which can give different forms of access to the information. These files can correspond in number and in character to all the different purposes which an archives service can have in requiring control of or access to its holdings. Some of these purposes are connected with internal management, the administrative control of the processes which have to be carried out on the material. Some are connected with exploitation, the intellectual control of the information held in the material.

The structure of data elements (given in the next chapter) sets out the data which may aptly appear in each of these categories. The data elements are listed in two parts, one part dealing with archival description and one with management control. The archival description sector contains the elements which are needed for intellectual control of the material, but embedded in these are the elements needed to write basic representations for the main file. The management information sector holds data elements which, when added to the main representation, give what is needed for administrative control.

The main and additional representation files do not necessarily consist of standard descriptions arranged in different orders: here is another important difference between archival and library practice. Not only is there a generic difference between descriptions at different levels but also a difference between the format of the data elements chosen for any particular file. Although the same data elements may appear in the central data base, their presentation in the finding aid must be planned in relation to the use that the finding aid is to be put to.

Finding aids in archives systems therefore consist of a main (structural) representation file, additional (subject-based) representation files, specialised files for administrative control, together with secondary information retrieval instruments, such as indexes and user guides, which bind the whole complex together.

Finding aid systems

The way the separate descriptions are put together constitutes the finding aid system of an archives service. It is best if the result is truly a system, in which the components are planned, and the linkages between them designed from the beginning. In real life, most collections of finding aids have grown up in response to particular needs in the past, and have not developed integrated linkages or common entry points.[2]

There is an appropriate form of description for archival entities at each level of arrangement. These descriptions can be combined in various ways. One main finding aid consists in their being put together in structural order, level by level. They may also be linked horizontally or vertically, and they may be linked by common or cross-referenced supporting retrieval instruments. Figure 11 shows these combinations.

A *horizontally* constructed finding aid is produced when an assembly of descriptions at the same range of levels is brought together. Putting together the group/collection or group and class descriptions relating to all the holdings of a repository results in a guide. The *Guide to the contents of the Public Record Office* is an assembly of macro descriptions of this kind. Each volume might be regarded as covering one archive group. Within the volumes, the guide is arranged in chapters, each of which corresponds to a group — generally the archives of a ministry or department. Each group description (containing subgroups in the text) is followed by all the class descriptions in that group, in logical or structural order. This results in a typical horizontal collection of descriptions, at all macro levels. Integration between the different parts is provided by

(a) a general introduction explaining the background to the accumulation, and the makeup of the holdings in general, and

(b) an index.

A *vertical* finding aid is created when the descriptions at

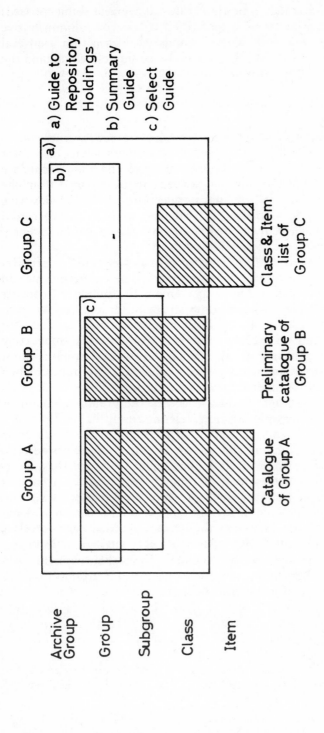

Figure 11 Horizontal and vertical finding aids

107

each level relating to a particular group/collection are assembled and produced as a single unit. This type of finding aid is usually called a catalogue. The *Londonderry papers*, published by the Durham Record Office is a good example, at least of a published version.[3] The catalogue consists of the group/collection description, then subgroups (and further divisions of the kind) in logical or structural order. Each subgroup description is used as a headnote for an item—level description which is given to quite a high degree of fullness. The whole is bound together by a general introduction, and by an index.

These two examples illustrate fairly common types of published finding aid. Where the descriptions are not published there is likely to be less integration. There is also scope for many more published aids of both horizontal and vertical kinds, for instance inter-repository guides, co-ordinated or combined indexes. Horizontal finding aids can include material selected on a subject basis (provided the level of description remains constant); or, less commonly, material selected on the basis of its diplomatic character or format. An example of the former is the PRO Handbooks series, *Records of interest to social scientists*,[4] and of the latter, collections of enclosure awards.[5] The Hampshire Archivists' Group publications, on school and poor law records, are perhaps intermediate between the two, but illustrate the possibility of inter-repository finding aids.[6]

The structure of archival descriptions

Archival finding aids are built up from descriptions which are essentially structured. They tend to contain two different kinds of component fields, those with free text or narrative entries, and those which are dedicated to specific data. It seems to be true of descriptions at all levels that there are fields of these two kinds present. At the upper levels of description, narrative text constitutes the main substance of the entry, and may be very long. Dedicated fields may seem relatively peripheral, and be confined to short entries such as the title and reference code. At the lower levels, item lists often have one free text field (the item title) which allows some freedom of description to the writer, but this field is usually embedded in a pattern of dedicated fields for reference code, dates, etc. At class level there is more of a balance. The main narrative description (called the abstract in the data elements) is supported by several dedicated fields for reference code, title, dates, bulk, condition, and so forth.

Since any archival entity, however small, ought generally to be described at two or more levels, there must be some way to link the two (or more) levels together vertically. Some record offices use the device of adding a title page to the description of each entity. The title pages could then be collected as a guide (this would be a horizontal finding aid); and they can also be used as an introduction to the lists that follow (this would be a vertical finding aid).

The concept of the title page, however, does not allow for all the situations in which there must be an explanatory macro description to introduce and govern a micro description. A more appropriate concept is that of the *headnote*. A headnote is any introductory entry which explains and controls a finding aid which appears below (or after) it, holds common information, and gives overall reference codes. In many cases the headnote is the related vertical macro description: thus a class description can serve as the headnote to an item list, or a group description to a class list. This can be done with any combination of levels. In other cases the headnote can be something written specially.

Sometimes the headnote appears clearly for what it is, standing at the head of the text of the micro description. At other times the function of the headnote is being discharged tacitly by an introduction or by a macro description, and in these cases the headnote may be separated from its dependent list. There must of course be some linking device to indicate the connection. Headnotes are a pervasive element in archival finding aid systems, and can take many forms.

There are some customary rules about the content of headnotes, but not about their format. They should always contain a statement which links the following material to its larger archival context, if any. They should contain a broad description of all material or information which is common to items in the governed assembly of material, so that it is not necessary to repeat information constantly in the list. (Unnecessary repetition is a common fault in archival micro descriptions). They should contain cross-references to related materials held elsewhere.[7]

Like all other archival descriptions, headnotes may consist of a free text field (the narrative information about what follows) accompanied by dedicated fields (reference code and title).

The central problem of archival description is that of depth, or fullness. It is clear that in most cases a representation does not contain all the information that is held in the original. If it did, it would be a facsimile: of course there is a role for facsimiles, but it is not as part of the system of finding aids. A set of representations which, while not being so full as actually to be facsimiles, but containing so much of the content of the originals that it can serve to replace them for virtually all purposes, is called a calendar. This is a case where the representation file becomes a surrogate file.

Many years ago, the main effort of archivists (in the field of description) was directed at making surrogate files. At first this was done by publishing full text transcripts. In the early years of the 19th century, before the foundation of the PRO, the publication of texts, as nearly as possible as facsimiles, was thought of as the main task. This work was taken so seriously that print conventions (record type) were introduced to improve the similarity between printed text and the originals of medieval manuscripts.[8] As time passed, economies were made by reducing the facsimiles to calendars, but these were still designed so that researchers could have direct access to the text in virtually all cases where it was perceived as important. American users can still quote the words of English Civil War generals, by consulting the *Calendar of State Papers Domestic* for the period.[9] Many of the finding aids produced since 1869 by the Royal Commission on Historical Manuscripts were produced on the same lines.[10]

In the later 20th century, archivists can rarely regard this type of publication as their first priority. Much more effort is put into the construction of more limited representation files, whose immediate objective is internal control. The best that can usually be offered to remote users is an indication of the likelihood or otherwise that there would be relevant items in a group.

One reason for this change is certainly that there are fewer resources in the face of growing commitments, but it is not clear to what extent we have abandoned or displaced the concept of the surrogate file available to remote users. Possibly the coming of different and more bulky types of archive has reduced the feasibility of full surrogation in any case. Even so, the continued publication of series such as *India: the Transfer of Power* show that the appeal of full text transcription has continued unabated in some quarters, and the willingness of governments and public bodies to pay for it still continues as well.[11] Even so, it is worth noting that this impressive series of full text publication is carried out by a specialist team, and is not regarded as part of the normal work of the archivists on the staff of the record office concerned. The construction of finding aids continues as an activity not directly linked to the publication of surrogate texts.

If full-text transcriptions and calendars can no longer be regarded as part of the main descriptive work of archivists, the question of the depth of description to be used in the finding aids which are produced remains a pressing one. A general principle might be that finding aids should be constructed at a depth of description which is the maximum possible in the circumstances. Finding aids should include rather than exclude data, and reductions in the depth of description should be justified by reference to planning decisions taken in the light of the service's priorities.

There are four kinds of constraint which operate to restrict the depth of description. The first of these is the nature of the materials being described. Many archives do not lend themselves to varying depths of description. There is, for example, very little that can be added to an item description like this:

[Headnote:] Schools Advisory committee.

AB1/1   Minute book   1964 Dec 5 − 1965 Jan 10

unless this is regarded as a case for the creation either of a surrogate, say by publishing the full text; or of an index to contents. In most cases, however, there is some intermediate possibility between these extremes. The archivist's business would be to decide how much to put in, and therefore what must be left out.

Secondly, there are the aims and objectives of the archive service and the archivist. The immediate purpose is to construct a finding aid which is to do a certain job, in administrative or intellectual control. The shape of the finding aid is determined by the nature of this purpose.

Thirdly, and most obviously today, there are constraints of staff time, skill and motivation. Most of the time spent in the arrangement and description of archives is spent in some form of research. Research is need to establish the provenance and original arrangement of the archives, to translate this into suitable levels of arrangement for management purposes, and then to identify subjects and persons important in the content of the material. This kind of analysis and research is the central professional expertise of archivists, and consequently it is the activity which gives most return in job satisfaction. To get it done demands not only that there should be time to do it, but also that there should be appropriately trained and talented staff members, and that they should want to do it. Motivation is connected with subject specialisation, and the desirability of allowing staff members to follow their preferred specialisms within the service. This is an important constraint.

Finally, there is the question of user needs and demands. If one defines the term 'user' broadly, this could be an overriding factor. Archival materials should, after all, be managed in such a way as to provide useful information where it is most needed. This may sometimes justify the construction of finding aids which are not much used at present, if it is expected that eventually they will be used, but in general one must imagine that an assessment of user needs will be made at the point where the finding aid system is being designed, or at least before embarking on a major listing exercise.[12]

Some of these constraints are more significant than others. In principle, lack of resources is the least important of them, since descriptions and control instruments should be made good enough to do the job they are intended to do. In the light of this, the most important thing is to understand the immediate objective of the listing exercise in the context of user needs. After this, the nature of the archive to be listed is the next most formative thing. Limitations of time and skill are the last consideration. However life seldom follows theoretical analyses of principle, and in practice what resources are available (within the framework of office priorities) may be a dominant consideration.

A common response to difficulties of resourcing is to introduce a system of two-stage listing: a quick brief list first, and return to do a fuller description later. This approach is quite common, and has been adopted as a policy by many archives services. However, there are many disadvantages in the two-stage approach. It is almost certain that the initial brief description will not produce a usable representation file for many purposes, and it is equally likely that the opportunity to return and make a fuller description will take a long time to come.

112

Many archivists feel that in principle it is better to adopt a policy of once-for-all processing, and to aim at a system in which each archival entity is given its final treatment as early as possible. Initial administrative controls can be established by means of an accessions registration: this gives some flexibility in the time-scale and allows priorities to be set. It is true, though, that there are dangers in this approach. Final archival arrangement demands research, and once it is established and reference codes attached to the documents, it is difficult to make any changes: a definitive description must be treated as final.

The next difficulty in establishing depth arises from the levels to be treated. Each level has an appropriate form of description, and of course each of these can be treated at different depths. Group descriptions are mainly narrative administrative histories: a bit of time devoted to research here is likely to produce quite lengthy essays on the development and significance of the organisation. R.B. Pugh's administrative history and analysis of the diplomatic of Colonial Office records is almost as long as the list to which it is an introduction. This may be regarded as a rather extreme example, even though this introduction is an important contribution to the academic study of modern diplomatic.[13] It would normally be possible to produce analytical introductions, and administrative histories, which contain less detail and yet continue to be useful for many purposes.

The structure of data elements attempts to suggest what are the irreducible contents of administrative and custodial histories, but these so much follow the nature of the material being described, that no general guide can be of much practical use.

Class descriptions also centre round a free text entry which can be of any length and must follow the material to be described. The data element structure suggests that sometimes it may be possible to set up an analysis of contents which could serve as a guide to the minimum data to be entered. Unfortunately there are not many such guides available, and most classes do not suit them.

The original analysis for setting up the data structure on this point was done in the archives section of the British Antarctic Survey in Cambridge. These archives contain, as one of their most important components, a series of technical reports on expeditions. They are fairly standard in character, and it is not too difficult to set up a grid which allocates boxes to data items such as geographical co-ordinates, name of expedition leader, purpose of research, etc. This works well in the BAS reports, but in other archives services, classes are usually too various to allow any sort of standard analysis of content. It does of course remain necessary to insist that free text abstracts should contain the keywords needed for indexing or search. The main function of a preset content analysis would be to ensure (if possible) that all relevant keywords were entered in it.

No structure of keyword analysis can be valid for all cases. It must remain a matter of choice (within the guidelines laid down by office policy) of the individual archivist, as to how fully the original material is to be represented by free text descriptions.

At item level much the same choice is likely to exist. Where the items are strongly uniform (as in a series of minute books or financial records) as much common information as possible goes into the headnote, and the remainder of the list can consist simply of volume numbers and covering dates. Even here there is a policy choice to be made, as the following example shows:

(a) [Headnote:] Advisory committee minute books, indexed.
    AB1/1   1964 Dec 5 − 1965 Jan 10
      /2   1965 Jan 11 − 1966 Mar 25 etc.

(b) [Headnote:] Advisory committee minute books, 13 vols, indexed.
    AB1/1−13 1964 − 1972.

For most purposes (b) would be a perfectly adequate finding aid. Users would be able to retrieve the volume they wanted by checking the dates of the minute books physically: brevity in the finding aid has to be made up by a secondary search on the shelves, but in cases like this, the secondary search would be justified. However it is possible to imagine circumstances in which a more precise retrieval from the list is required, for instance if ordering by remote users is envisaged, or if the material listed is more complex.

In a list of file (dossier) titles, much more discretion is possible. If a dossier has a title, this should be checked for accuracy and fullness, for it is notorious that original file titles can be very misleading. Indexes are drawn from the free text fields of item lists also, and therefore the main need is that the right keywords should be there.

A good deal of difficulty is experienced in shortening the descriptions given to collections of title deeds. Traditionally it was common to give deeds a full, or almost full, calendar, which included a mention of the three main variables used in research reference:

the date and nature of the transaction recorded;
the names and designations of parties;
topographical details.

The advent of short descriptions meant that calendaring of individual deeds tended to give way to bulk descriptions of whole bundles:

DBT3/4—23   19 deeds relating to Ambridge.   1560—1900.

This example of bulk listing is almost certainly too brief for most users. The secondary search that would be required to identify relevant documents or information is disproportionate to the time saved in the original listing. Some compromise is needed.

The solution would doubtless be to approach the description of the bundle of deeds in the same spirit of management in which a filing system would be approached in RM. The aim would be to give an overall control of the materials by mastering the major facts about the composition and content of the class. This involves reading the documents at least rapidly, and making a summary of the sequence of events, main parties (including their connection with each other), and a locally identifiable note of the properties involved. A description of this kind exercises traditional archival skills, involves some research, and produces a result usable in further research. It takes time and skill resources, but less time than a full calendar would have done. The result will be a two-level description which includes something like an administrative history at the macro level, and a brief list at the micro level.

Overall, there should be enough in descriptions to give some assurance that a user would be able to make a correct assessment of the character and likely content of the entity being described, and be sure that all applicable keywords have appeared in the index. Major areas of omission (whether arising from policy or not) should be indicated somewhere, in order to avoid introducing a bias.

There is a broad inverse ratio between levels of arrangement and depth of description. This is natural, considering that the higher the level of arrangement and description, the larger is the number of archive entities being covered in the one description. Equally, the larger the proportion of the description that is permitted in free text, the less will be the fullness of detail (see Figure 12).

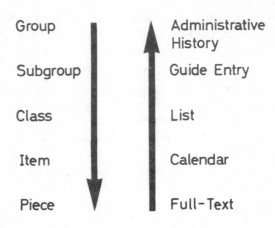

Group	Administrative History
Subgroup	Guide Entry
Class	List
Item	Calendar
Piece	Full-Text

Figure 12 Depth and level: relationships

There may well be considerable variety of depth in a single finding aid. The standard example is that of the archives of a landed estate. This may contain medieval deeds of title, which it has been customary to calendar (when before 1300 in very full detail); modern title deeds which receive a less full treatment but still one which mentions type of transaction, names of parties and details of the property conveyed; estate rentals or surveys which cannot be summarised; correspondence; and administrative notes. The date range of a single series can be from, say 1500 to, say 1900. In these circumstances it is normal to describe items at varying depths. In other circumstances, uniformity of depth at least within the same group would be an important objective.

1. *Accruals*

The problem of accruals is more awkward in the area of description than it is in the area of management. A class which receives many new accruals need not be stored together as a physical unit, but must have a description which will allow it to be understood and accessed as a whole. The case of a class which receives annual new consignments is an example. If the new annual addition is listed separately, users must either know exactly the year they wish to search, or they must consult several year-lists. Related items may well recur through the lists for several years. Yet to integrate the lists without integrating the materials physically also leads to trouble, for constant renumbering, both in the lists and on the shelves and containers, or on the documents themselves, would be difficult. The same problem occurs in a records management context.

It is not possible to suggest a complete solution. H.A. Taylor hints that there is such a thing as a 'natural' size to a class, by which is meant, perhaps, that archival divisions should correspond to manageable units as well as to organisational or functional distinctions in the material.[14] Those in charge of the management of new accruals may take advantage of any change in the administrative status of the originating office, to close the old class and open a new one — but this cannot be done too often, for the advantages of continuity in a class usually outweigh those of keeping the size of classes down.[15]

It may be possible to undertake a periodical reassessment, which would be accompanied by a partial rewriting of the macro description. This would mean that the overall description of the class would include successively received material, and would make this plain to the user. However, as the micro descriptions and reference codes would be left unaltered, the user would still have to scan all the successive lists of accrued material.

Rewriting the macro description would have less effect on the indexes than would a rearrangement of the micro lists. All the same, amending indexes is a tiresome business and much prone to omissions and errors. The effect of these problems is illustrated in MAD, Part IV.

2. Bias

It is safe to assert that archival finding aids are honestly meant, and are not intended to deceive. It is not so certain that their honest purpose is always achieved. Since the effectiveness of any representation file depends on the suitability of the representation, it will hardly be surprising if there are cases of poor representation or inadequate notation of important features. This leads to bias in the finding aids.

Normally the danger of bias arises from of the omission of data which should be there, rather than from the inclusion of redundant data, but cases of both could certainly be found. If data is omitted, it cannot be found by any ordinary user technique, and could not feature in the indexes. On the other hand, if a lot of irrelevant data is included in the finding aids, users are discouraged from systematic scanning, and indexes may be choked.

A useful illustration of this last point was provided in a discussion meeting which brought up a case where the place-names appendent on personal names of parties to title deeds had been indexed.[16] This had introduced a bias into the place-name index, because of the admission of a large number of names which had no immediate topographical relevance. The appearance of John Jones of Yardley, husbandman, in an 18th century marriage settlement, does not constitute a useful place-name reference to Yardley; at least not for ordinary purposes.

The distortion of a representation through the omission of data is much easier to illustrate. The brief description of a bundle of deeds given above can be used. A closer examination of this bundle may show that the majority of deeds refers more to the marriage and investment policy of the Archer family than to the transfer of lands in Ambridge. If this is so, then the description is misleading as well as unhelpfully brief.

Bias may also arise from confusion between levels of description in a single finding aid. If, for example, class and item descriptions are brought together in a list, one result may be that a user may lose his way:

ART16/24 Student withdrawals 1964—1978
FIN83/20 Medical Research Council grant 17992, 1978—9
FIN83/21 Science Research Council grant 0661, 1980.

In this example of part of an RM transfer list, the first record refers to a class (or perhaps to an accrual to a class), while the

118

second two describe items. The distinction will be clear only to those familiar with the system, or to those who access the material and find that the first entry produces several boxes of material, but each of the others only one slim dossier. The first entry could have a second-level extension:

ART16/24   Student withdrawals 1964—1978
    Box 1   Students A—H
    Box 2   Students J—Z.

Another important cause of bias could be the lack of uniformity in depth of description, but this has already been discussed. Finding aids produced over many years commonly vary in this way. The early ones may be excessively detailed, the later ones too brief. There may have been variations in depth at different times, because of staff shortages, or periods of crisis. These variations can have important consequences for the success of searches, and the confidence of users in the finding aid system. If users put too much trust in the system, they may lose information just as much as when they do not trust it enough. A periodical survey of the continuities of the system may often be justified.

The essential rule is that a representation should be accurate for the purposes of the specific finding aid it is used in. An inaccurate reference code, for instance, might not be very important in a group description, where it could be checked against other codes relating to components of the group. An inaccuracy in the reference code in an RM transfer list, however, could well result in the loss of the document. No doubt it would be desirable if information were always accurate, but there is a scale of relative values. Some inaccuracies are more destructive than others.

Multi-repository finding aids

The possibility of a system of inter-repository finding aids, amounting eventually to a national system, has become increasingly attractive of recent years, especially in view of the progress achieved in the USA. Neither the National Union Catalog of Manuscript Collections (NUCMC) nor the national directory of repositories of the USA has been exactly paralleled in Britain.[17]
There are some examples of local inter-repository guides, such as the Hampshire Archivists' Group publications, or the series of lists of West Midlands archives services produced as a

newsletter. These publications have not yet reached the scale and standard of published reports produced by specialised surveys of source materials. These include the volumes of the British Political Records survey.[18] On a less elaborate scale, the reports of the Contemporary Scientific Archives survey might be mentioned, although there are many others.[19]

The publications and finding aids produced by the Royal Commission on Historical Manuscripts increasingly suggest a slow movement towards a national finding aid system.[20] This has recently been supplemented by the commercially published micro-form edition of an inventory of documentary sources.[21]

A pilot scheme for a computerised inter-repository listing system, PROSPEC-SA, achieved a degree of technical success in the late 1970s, but was abandoned for lack of central funding. The chief potential of this scheme was the production of a multi-repository version of finding aids which already existed in individual archives services. Its abandonment suggests that there is not as yet a strong impetus towards the creation of widely ranging catalogues and guides.[22]

The problems inherent in constructing multi-repository finding aids are now well known. They centre upon two areas: the compatibility of the finding aids as between repositories, and the need to introduce new retrieval instruments to support the new multi-repository finding aids.

Compatibility within and between repositories would demand, for example, that levels of description should be correctly analysed, and suitable models taken for both depth and level. It is fairly certain that in most cases these have not been consistent in the past, even where they are so in the case of newly constructed finding aids.

Putting descriptive materials together in composite forms highlights the need to create new indexes to them. The new indexes need structured vocabularies. This might be a questionable statement if it referred only to the holdings of one repository. The experience of PROSPEC-SA however was unmistakeable. It showed that a thesaurus was needed if a joint machine-generated finding aid was to be viable. It is difficult to fund this work, precisely because it lies outside the direct needs of any particular repository. Moreover the value of the multi-repository finding aids can only be truly assessed from a national and not from a repository standpoint. It is clear that a national scheme for wide-ranging finding aids will not succeed unless it is organised nationally and seen as a national asset.

National and international bibliographic systems

This chapter began with an attempt to compare library and archival descriptions. Its conclusion was that although there are important common principles, their application in practice is radically different. This conclusion is reinforced when the question of compatibility between archival descriptions and national or international standards of bibliographic description is considered.

Within the nation, and within library and documentation systems, there is a fair degree of acceptance that bibliographic standards have been established by AACR2, which includes chapters both on manuscripts and on non-book materials.[23] Much book cataloguing is now organised on an inter-repository basis, and progress has been made with computerised bibliographical descriptions. Standards for this have been established by MARC, which again includes specialised formats for manuscripts and NBM.[24]

These developments have been extended by the creation of a number of electronic data bases, which allow users remote access, either on-line to relevant documents, or to bibliographies through which they can gain access to relevant documents by the use of national library networks, inter-library loans, etc. Some of these data bases, including for example the national bibliography itself (BNB), have developed sophisticated indexing systems which have the appearance at least of being compatible with archival indexing: for example the system known as PRECIS.[25]

There has been a considerable degree of international linkage in the bibliographical field, especially where electronic data bases and formats are concerned. There are international standards of compatibility, under the heading of the International Standard Book Description (ISBD), and Common Communications Format (CCF).[26] Specific standards for various types of material, particularly technical documentation, have been established, and the MARC formats, although split into national types as between North America and Britain, do operate as an international standard.

In the USA, much progress has been made in developing comparable standards for archival description. Finding both the AACR2 and the MARC standard unworkable, groups of archivists have rewritten both. S.L. Hensen has produced a model revision of AACR2.[27] RLIN is now in operation as an on-line electronic data base containing archival material in several repositories.[28]

Most archivists, at work within their own repositories, are not actively conscious of the progress of this kind of co-operative work. Those who are most concerned with the development of common standards, and particularly archivists within large library and museum services, have nevertheless made some effort to assess the problems and to begin work on comparable standards and practices for archival description.[29]

The question is, have they been successful? Certainly there have been successful ventures in the co-operative exchange of archival information, especially in North America. It is probably true to say, however, that up to the present it has not been possible to produce a standard for archival description which is adapted from AACR2 or any of its derivatives, and which has been widely accepted by archivists as a useful tool for ordinary purposes within repositories. The Archival Description Project which worked at Liverpool University during 1984—5 took this view, and suggested in its report that there would be scope for further research on seeking to develop an AACR2-compatible standard.[30]

Some of the reasons for the difficulties enountered have been outlined in earlier parts of this chapter, and the fact that these difficulties are not always appreciated by librarians tends to make the problem more difficult. The increasing demand for international standards and provision for immediately accessible data bases makes it important for us to reach for solutions. It is not acceptable that library and archival standards for the description of their materials should continue to be so irreconcilable.

User response

It is probable that no considered effort has ever been made to investigate the user response to archival finding aids, in the context of any British archive service, nor have user organisations attempted to concentrate on this aspect. Although there would be many difficulties in implementing it, an extensive user study is clearly overdue.[31]

It was mentioned earlier in this chapter that the main representation file should be a structural one, but that this type of finding aid was not usually user-friendly. A structural finding aid is directly and immediately useful only to one type of user, a researcher who is studying the origin and central development of the organisation whose archives are under inspection. Such a user will be looking primarily for evidential material. Other users, who wish to use informational material, will find the structural finding aid of marginal value, and will find the administrative history which it contains necessary but tiresome.

On the other hand, it is not entirely clear that the majority of users would prefer subject-based finding aids. R.H. Lytle's 1979 study tested the reliability of retrieval from structural and subject-based descriptions (this, of course, is not quite the same question) and came to the conclusion that neither system had much advantage over the other.[32] This meant that since structural listings must necessarily continue to be the main description (for reasons of moral defence), there is no pressing reason why traditional approaches should be changed. Probably there is a need for more subject-based descriptions, so that finding aid systems should perhaps be designed with their possibility in mind. Subject-based finding aids (incorporating an element of the structural) may be produced by assembling sets of subgroup or class descriptions on a selective basis.

Users certainly need indexes to find their way into finding aids, and would probably voice a preference for union indexes which integrate finding aid systems, provided these were properly designed.

Archival descriptions, at whatever level, should be formatted with user needs in mind. In particular, users need to scan lists for specific information, and therefore the fields used in them should be laid out accordingly. A user scanning for relevant dates, for instance, would be grateful to have covering dates set out in a separate column on the left of the free text field. Free text, on the other hand, lends itself to browsing, the main other user technique for dealing with the identification of material.

Finding aids are part of the outreach or publication programmes of the archives service. One consequence of this is that there should be a clear decision on their openness to users. Ideally, all finding aids should be classified as for free access, even where they relate to originals which are closed. (In this case, there would be a note in the finding aids stating access conditions.) Ideally too, a version of every significant description should be found in the National Register of Archives.

In practice, these counsels of perfection are probably unattainable, since it is sometimes necessary to conceal either the fact of custody of certain materials, or at least some details about them. It would still be preferable if the principle of openness were to be adopted explicitly, and provision made for certain exceptions.

The structure of data elements in archival description

The Society of Archivists began holding annual in-service courses in computing in 1982. By that time groups of archivists had begun to prepare for what seemed the imminent age of the computer by preparing an analysis of the structure of data elements in archival description. The Methods of Listing working party (of the Specialist Repositories Group of the Society) had already been at work on this for a year. The working party produced a draft data structure, and this was examined at a series of open meetings held at a variety of places, and finally reached a 6th version. At this stage (1984) the Archival Description Project at Liverpool University, which was working on a standard for non-computerised archival description, took up the work and incorporated the data structure into its *Manual of Archival Description* (MAD).[1] Some American models were influential at this stage (particularly that of the Research Libraries Group).[2]

The Methods of Listing working party perceived that its main task was to produce an analysis of the data elements which together constitute a full archival description; they had also to compile a kind of classification scheme to govern the relationships between these data elements. This was achieved by the final version of the working party's data standard and, in an alternative form, in the first edition of MAD. A summary of this second version is given below.

Summary of the General Structure of Data Elements

I. *Archival description sector*

1. Identity (obligatory field)

2. Administrative and custodial history

> Administrative history
> Originating administrator/office
> Place of origin
> Administrative authority
> Dates

Custodial history
  Ownership changes
  Places of custody
  Transfer to archives
  Funding
  Dates
  Obsolete reference codes

3. Archival description

  Title
  Abstract
    Contents analysis
  Diplomatic description
    Original indexes
    Predominant language
    Characteristic script

4. Physical description

  Form and extent
  Copies
  Condition
  Special features

5. Access, publication and reference record (joint with Management Information sector)

  Access and copyright
  Publication record
  Related materials
  Exhibition record

II. *Management information sector*

1. Administrative control information

  Acquisition/accession control
    Accession code
    Date and method of acquisition
    Immediate source/provenance
    Bulk
    Funding

  Location
    Place of storage
    Measurement of space occupied
    Accrual rate

2. Internal movement control

> Control of processing
> Completion of archival description
> Indexing
> Production of archive for reference by users
> Reference to archive in answer to enquiries
> Loan record
> Appraisal review

3. Conservation record.

The summary given above shows that the General Structure of Data Elements is divided into two main parts, one dealing with data needed for the identification and retrieval of archival entities and the information within them, and the other covering management information.

It is not entirely possible to divide all the data elements neatly into these two categories: in practice, archival finding aids get used both for internal administration and for providing a service to readers. One of the components of the archival description sector, entitled the access, publication and reference record, in fact belongs about equally to both sectors, and should perhaps have been treated as an independent element.

It should also be noted that the basic archival description, formatted to suit the appropriate level, is needed as much for management information as for intellectual control. The two sectors of the data element structure are interdependent in this respect.

The Archival Description Sector

This sector is divided into three areas, and so at first sight resembles the areas of information provided for bibliographic descriptions in AACR2.[3] After a closer acquaintance, the resemblance tends to become superficial, since none of the data elements themselves really corresponds at all closely with those used in bibliographical cataloguing.

There is an ambiguity in the terminology of the archival description sector. The elements of the whole sector are needed to provide the description of any archive entity, while at the same time there is a section labelled 'archival description'. In fact, the latter only indicates one of the main fields within the description of an archival entity, though its relative importance varies according to the levels being described. This point will be difficult for non-archivists to understand, for the section 'archival description' may tend to look rather like the bibliographical description in a book cataloguing system. The difficulty will be better understood when the models for description at the various levels of arrangement are examined.

An accumulation of archives is sorted, and arranged in component groupings according to level. The description process then deals with these level by level. The group as a whole has a description proper to itself, which concentrates on the circumstances which brought the group into existence. The historical survey continues through the subgroups. The description of classes which comes next appears to move a little closer to bibliographical practice, in that it is a series of class-by-class descriptions, which might be compared with a library catalogue. Finally there are lists of items, which do not look at all bibliographical. A completed set of hierarchical finding aids therefore consists of at least three (and probably at least four, in practice) levels of description, each of which has a model of its own.

The first area in the sector is compulsory for all archival descriptions, and is a statement of the *identity* of the archival entity (at whatever level, or of whatever size) that is being described. Generally, identity is established by means of an archival reference code, though there are cases when a plain-language title could be used instead, especially for large groups. Reference codes usually refer the user to the level of description being used. Titles can also suggest level, and indeed the importance of titles decreases, in archival description, as one passes from the higher to the lower levels.

The next area is called the *administrative, and custodial history* of the archival entity being described. One of the higher levels of description is envisaged here, though of course every archival entity has both an administrative and a custodial history, which may be important in its interpretation. This history can have two aspects, and both form a part of the full description. Firstly there is the administrative history of the organisation which brought the archive group or class into being; and secondly there is the custodial history — the history of the events which have occurred in the life of that archive between its original creation and (an important event which normally should always be recorded) its passing into the regular custody of the archives service.

The various elements which might go into an administrative history are set out in the data standard. They include the name and function of the administrator or administrative unit, office or person who was responsible originally for creating the archive, the place where the creation and original storage was done (and if relevant, the department or sub-organisation which was responsible), and the authority under which the creators were acting at the time. This provision has in mind principally the case of records generated as a result of legislation or a formal decision of the governing body of an organisation, but the provision could be relevant also to the records of a private individual. In this case, the authority statement could refer to an event or undertaking in the person's life, such as joining an official committee or taking up some enterprise.

The administrative history inevitably includes some description of the functions intended to be carried out (or actually carried out — this may be different) by the creating organisation. This makes the administrative history an important first guide to the user, who can use it to assess the likely relevance of the group or subgroup to the intended researches.

The custodial history refers to the archive's adventures in the period after it ceased to be in current use as a business record until after its transfer to or deposit in the archives service. There will always be at least one event in this history, the transfer itself. Often, there will be much more. The adventures of many groups of British government archives in the long period between their currency and their eventual arrangement in a public repository were colourful, and had visible effects on the physical appearance of the material. Some of the State Papers ended up in the British Museum, and played a part in the development of that repository as a centre of research, and as a national institution.[4]

The treatment of the archives in the light of their custodial history may also have a bearing on their value as primary evidence. We no longer believe, as Jenkinson did, that an archive's value in research or as legal evidence depends on our certainty that it has never left official custody: primary sources are evaluated as to their authenticity (i.e. tests can be made to see that they are not forgeries, or have not been altered), not as to the purity of their custodial history.[5] Nevertheless the custodial history is of interest in the interpretation of the documents, and should be set out in the

129

main description of the group.

Custodial history may record the sequence of ownership changes, both those which left the archive *in situ*, and those (such as changes by sale) which involved the material being moved, and perhaps its arrangement disturbed. The place of the owner's custody, or the sequence of these places, may be valuable information. Generally, there should be some information on the conditions under which the transfer to the archives service took place, whether by transfer under statute or official regulation, deposit by a private owner, bequest, purchase or rescue; and of course the date of this transaction. Finally the trail of clues which points to the course of the custodial history — the original or other obsolete reference codes which the documents may have borne — could be indicated. (The detail of this particular point might be more appropriate in a micro description.) It is possible that there may be cases where the transfer section of the custodial history may have to be kept confidential.[6]

The administrative and custodial history area can be regarded as the main component of a macro description — particularly at group or subgroup level. At this level, some additions on the physical character of the archive, and a reference to the whereabouts of appropriate micro descriptions would probably complete it as a working finding aid. Alternatively, though, the area can be regarded as forming part of an archival description, the most central part of which is the area which follows.

This area, the *archival description* itself, is the one which corresponds most closely, in its general appearance and make-up to a catalogue entry for books. Like all the forms mentioned in the data standard, this one can be used at any level, but takes its most characteristic shape at class level: that is, at the point where the micro descriptions meet the higher-level ones, the point of greatest importance where management needs are concerned.

The archival description consists of a central free text field (the narrative description itself, termed in the data structure the abstract) linked to a number of dedicated or fixed fields. Logically the description field is a double one, containing a title and an abstract. Since archival items, let alone classes or groups, do not normally have titles in the sense in which published materials have, the title usually is something derived by the archivist from the archive entity itself. The title of a group will normally be the title of the creating organisation, with suitable qualifiers.

Subgroups bear the names of the functional subdivisions to which they refer. When classes are being dealt with it may be necessary to supply a title by examining their make-up and content. To find a suitable title, the archivists will first look for evidence as to whether the class had a title, or some sort of working label, when it was in current use. If this approach fails, alternative sources are form ('the Red Book(s)'), function ('registers of vaccinations'), place of original custody ('Leahurst correspondence files'), name of original compiler ('Lord Smith's in-letters'). If these elements fail to produce a satisfactory title, then recourse can be had to the reference code. It is essential that an archival entity should be related to its context, particularly in regard to level, but it can do without a title.

MAD recommends that titles should contain at least two of three possible elements: a personal or corporate name; a term indicating the form of the material; and covering dates. This recommendation originated in proposals for cataloguing rules within a manuscript library, and one can see that they have in mind the kind of title often adopted by libraries for their manuscript collections. A typical example would be 'Alexander Hamilton papers, 1757—1804'.[7] The recommendation is perhaps less suitable for a public archives service, since both the form and the date parameters may be unnecessary. Even so, a group title such as 'Borough of Borchester' [*sc* official archives], c1560—1835' would be perfectly acceptable in this context. Close alternatives such as 'Borough of Borchester before the Municipal Reform Act' would satisfy the recommendation just as well.

After the title comes the abstract, a free text narrative description. It is important that the abstract should contain all the data items in the original which would be required for effective retrieval. It is likely that the abstract will be the source of any keywords used in a search, whether that were to be a manual or an on-line search. To ensure that these keywords are included, it may be useful to provide the archivist with a series of prompts, in the form of fixed subfields to be filled in with specific data where it occurs. These specific items might include dates (single or covering); site, locality or place (in some situations map co-ordinates could be used); personal names; events or activities; or subject keywords generally. Since it is likely that this will be the source of any index, it is important to provide the necessary basic infrastructure of permitted vocabulary for these key terms. For instance many record offices provide a list of place names within the county, hierarchically arranged under ancient parishes; there may be rules governing the form of personal names. Subject wordlists or thesauri are less common, but sometimes a wider subject keyword list can be used, such as SHIC.[8]

The dedicated fields linked to the free text sections are variable in their fullness. Some may have relatively lengthy entries, while some can be limited to a narrow range of possible data. Diplomatic description is a field which must allow considerable variation. It should give some information on the form of the record: at group level this will be brief, but at class and item levels some free text may be needed (e.g. class: correspondence filing systems; loose-leaf registers. Item: mortgage, marriage settlement, letter). As mentioned above, a word or two from the diplomatic description may be used as one of the elements in the title, and if this is done, then of course it need not be repeated. This section can be used to note the existence of any original indexes or finding aids, since these may be important means of access to the archive.

Another field allows for a note of problems encountered in relation to this archive, such as missing information, difficulty of interpretation, or the like. Narrower fields are those which can be used to note the predominant language used, and the characteristic script ('Chancery hand'), where this information is important. All these fields can apply to descriptions at all levels, though the way in which they are used varies according to the level.

The next area of the data standard contains a *physical description*. This provides space for a note on the formal character of the archive: files, volumes, bundles (this may be replaced by or linked with the note on diplomatic character in the preceding section). Next comes data on dimensions, material, quantity, text (sometimes a link with the predominant script is indicated). A note of the existence of any copies, microfilm, photocopy, transcript, and so on, may appear here, and then a brief statement of the physical condition of the class, especially where this might affect the archivist's decision on whether or not to allow access. The area is completed with entries containing information on special features, such as seals, watermarks, or any other physical feature which may be worthy of study, or which might affect access. Once again, this area may be used at any level, but increases in specificity at the lower levels.

The next area is called the *access, publication and reference record*, and is intermediate between the archival description sector and the management information sector. It contains data which is needed for the construction of public finding aids, and also for the management of processes within the repository.

The access field is used to record any limitations on the openness of access there may be, either general limitations applicable to all users, or limitation to some particular group of users. These limitations may take the form of an action date associated with the general closure period. An example which is of value equally for public users and for archivists managing the user services is the case where access becomes open after thirty years, and the action date is 25 March 1950: the material becomes open at 26 March 1980 (or, more usually in practice, on 1 January 1981).

There may be restrictions on reproduction of the material, which again may allow for privileged users (such as authorised representatives of the originating department). Relevant data here has a management context: a cross-reference to correspondence files recording policy instructions on access and reproduction limitations may be useful.

A third field allows the extension of this information to the question of copyright. It may be necessary to record the ownership of the copyright, restrictions imposed on users through copyright, its expiry date, and cross-reference to the office's correspondence files.

Both intellectual and administrative control demands that there should be information on the publication history of an archive. The reference may include a correct bibliographic description of a published version of an archival text, or a reference to a case where the archive has been cited. These are sometimes complicated questions, especially where the data item is being included in a group or subgroup description, and there may be need for some freedom to insert textual notes.

Linked with the publication record is a field which allows for a reference to associated materials: archives or published work, perhaps based on the holdings of a different repository, which bears upon the content or interpretation of the archives. This should hold at least the relevant cross-reference and a free-text note of the nature of the relationship.

Whether an archival entity has at some stage been lent out for exhibition may be a point of interest to public users, and is certainly a point which requires management information. Exhibition is a form of publication. A proper record of it might include the name of the person or organisation to whom the material was lent, the dates of the loan, and a reference to any formal publication or reference in the exhibition catalogue.

This completes the archival description sector, and the remainder of the data standard constitutes the management information sector. Its main purpose is to record information useful for the internal management of the archives service, the establishment of administrative controls over the material, and the control of the various processes through which the archives are put.

Management Information Sector

The management information sector contains three areas, covering administrative control information, internal movement control, and conservation.

Administrative control information has two broad divisions. In the first, information about the acquisition of the archive is recorded. Fields provided ask for data on its accession (this may refer to a separate accessions register). The date of this event is an important item, and so are its means of acquisition and its immediate provenance or source. Means of acquisition could include purchase, gift, loan, deposit, transfer or rescue; this field links with final event noted in the custodial history. Because there will probably be data here which ought not to be published at first or without restriction, a separate section for management use is provided. It is important that there should be a permanent record. To complete administrative control, there should be provision for information on the bulk of the accession, and any arrangements for managing future accruals, This may suggest a 'bring-forward' record reminding the staff to make contact with the originating organisation at a certain date, giving reference to the relevant correspondence files, and to the source of funding where this exists.

The second division provides for a location record, and a tool for the management of the space occupied. The place of storage is obviously necessary as a finding aid. The volume of storage or shelving occupied also suggests a need for information on the expected rate of accrual and the expected date of the next consignment.

The *internal movement control* area contains seven divisions, all concerned with the supervision of processes carried out within the archives service, and not of direct concern to users. The first division provides a control of the completion of the main processes: these are broadly termed archival and physical arrangement of the material. Within this broad label are included a host of operations, ranging from initial registration, through fumigation, boxing, labelling, through to final completion of the finding aids. The amount of detail given in the record depends on the level (primarily chosen for management convenience) and the nature of the material. The identity of the archivist responsible, whether there was any separate funding, and the dates of completion of the different stages, may be recorded here.

At the end of all this, the completion of the final archival description, with the name of the staff member responsible, a note of funding and the date, may be a useful record. A similar record may be provided for the completion of the indexing work, though this of course may be regarded as integral to the general description.

A record of production of the material for reference by a user has a division of the data standard. This record might have fields for the user's identity and for the circumstances of the access given. The designers of the data standard intended that this part of it should be usable in the context of RM, and therefore there are fields covering the issue and return of material to internal users, and for recording the number of times a record entity is referred to in any given period. The number of times a class is accessed in a year, for instance, may be significant when it is being appraised, or when the retention schedule is being revised. Access to the record, and its issue to users, should be governed by a policy in regard to that actual category of record, and therefore it should be possible to include a cross-reference to documents or sources laying down what this policy is.

Another division is used to record cases where reference to the archive has been made in order to answer enquiries from outside users. The full record could include the identity of the enquirer, the date of the reference, and a means of identifying the appropriate correspondence in the files. Perhaps it should be added that because the data standard makes provi-

135

sion for this kind of record, it must not be taken as advocating that this record should always be kept. Whether this is done or not is a question to be decided by the archives service itself, bearing in mind its general needs and resources. Many archives services quite clearly do not record enquiry references to their material, and do not keep the enquiries themselves.

Loan of material for use in exhibitions or for reference in another repository, where it happens, makes it necessary to have a control record. Fields needed might include the name of the person or organisation to which the loan was made, the dates of sending out and return (or the date on which return is due), and a note of insurance requirements. This division refers back to the record of exhibition loans which is part of the publication record.

The last division is primarily for RM information and provides for appraisal reviews. This notes the appraisal category or the action to be taken, the date on which action is due, and the officer responsible for it. There might well have been further provision here, for RM procedures in connection with review might include sending a disposal recommendation to the originating department, recording a disposal instruction, or varying the policy in special cases. If these items, or any like them, are to be included, they could come in this area of the data standard.

The final area provides a *conservation record*, which is to be a permanent part of the archive's custodial history, and also an administrative control over repair processes. This area could be used to preserve a record of previous conservation history, and of repair work needed and carried out. The conservator responsible, start and finish dates, and return to permanent storage, all have dedicated fields. Another field might be used to bring the item forward for inspection or further repair at a stated date. Another use of this record might be to help with stock control by recording the use of materials in repair: this may of course be cross-referenced to conservation registers in use in the service. If there is special funding this may be noted.

The data items in the management information sector can be applied to any level of arrangement or description, but a movement down the scale to class and item can be perceived in the later areas and divisions. It is probable that most physical controls are best exercised at class level, but that the conservation record may tend to descend to item level at times. Even here, however, it is worth recalling that environmental conservation, being a management function, should probably seek to find a level well above item for its main operation. Environmental conservators should look to class (if not subgroup) as their main level of control, and therefore will need to frame their finding aids and control instruments accordingly.

The full detail of the general structure of data elements, instructions on applying them to particular archival descriptions, a set of model descriptions, and examples, are given in MAD, Parts III and IV.

Information retrieval in archival systems

In order to plan and co-ordinate finding aid systems in archival management it will be useful to use some of the principles and practices of information retrieval. In this chapter two areas are examined for the possible relevance of some of these to the management of information held in archives. These are indexing and searching.

In practice, most archives services have tended to use indexes of the end-of-volume type, and indexes on cards. Other physical types, such as sheaf indexes, are less common, and the use of electro-mechanical card systems is negligible. Automated indexes of any kind are not common at present, but deserve discussion because of their potential for the future.

Irrespective of their physical form, indexes are a necessary component of any finding aid, and therefore of any finding aid system. The distinction between these two things is important, for on the conceptual level there are clearly two kinds of index to be met with in an archival system. One kind is the index to a specific finding aid: in some cases the index may itself be the principal finding aid to some part of the holdings. The other kind is the index to the macro descriptions generally. An example would be the index(es) to the guide. These provide one of the two possible initial entry points for users, and are an essential linkage between parts of the system. The first kind has to be very specific in its construction and its entries, the second must be constructed on a broader model, so that the amalgamation of different indexes of the same kind can be considered.

Initial entry points

The distinction between specific and general indexes may serve to introduce a discussion of the initial entry points in archival description systems. Users beginning a search must make their entry into the finding aids either from the top (the widest possible view of the subject) or from the bottom (the narrowest and most detailed view). In this analysis, entry from the top means using the guide first, with its index; the terms searched for may be the broader ones in a structured indexing scheme, and the user will be looking for the most appropriate groups to search. Entry from the bottom would mean searching for specific or narrower terms in the index to a particular group or archival entity as a way of scanning the item or class lists: the user's objective would be the identification of individual documents. These two approaches are not total alternatives, for the user's strategy is determined by the nature of the search being undertaken, and the amount of background knowledge the user already has. Indexes are available as a starting point at both levels:

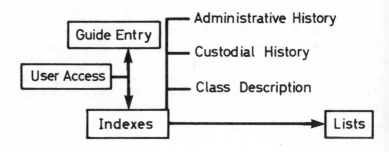

The difference between library and archive practice is particularly obvious in this area. In libraries, the subject index normally forms part of the principal representation file, the catalogue, or else is a separate and parallel catalogue. In an archival finding aid system, the principal representation file is normally something quite distinct from any form of index. The guides, catalogues and lists of an archival finding aid system are distinct in format and intention from the indexes which provide one way of entry into their textual contents. An exception to this is the one mentioned above, the case where the index is itself the main finding aid to a particular group. Lionel Bell discusses this case in his important article of 1971.[1]

Another point of difference is that in archival searching the names and designations of particular persons and administrative structures in the originating organisation are especially important as guides to the whereabouts of subject information.[2] To identify which subgroup or class is most relevant to a search, a user often needs only to establish which office or person was responsible for a relevant function during the

140

period of currency. A full administrative history ought to reveal the most useful names. After discovering these, the user may be able to build a search strategy on retrieving the names of functionaries, wherever they occur at appropriate dates. It follows that many subject enquiries can be answered, at least for skilled users, by reference to institutional or personal name indexes.

> The arrangement of archives by provenance goes a good deal of the way to narrow the field in record enquiries. In respect of any one enquiry nearly all administrative departments can be ruled out on chronological grounds, or those of area of competence in a way which is not paralleled in the library field.[3]

Index references are normally to keywords in the main finding aids, and not directly to data held in the original archive materials, The MAD data structure for archival description proposes that the central descriptive feature should be a free text abstract. Free text descriptions also occur in administrative/custodial histories and in all headnotes — that is, they form the bulk of all macro descriptions. They also appear in some fields in micro descriptions, for instance where there are dossier titles. All these fields should be capable of providing material for index construction, which means that they should ideally be written with the aid of a thesaurus or permitted vocabulary, and should contain all the necessary terms for transposal to the index.

Special indexing problems arise where medieval or other early archives are the subject of the index. These include spelling variants, obsolete or changing name forms, illegible or difficult readings, and the need to identify names, places and specialised terms. The main problems here are discussed in specialist studies.[4]

Indexes as the principal finding aid

The possibility that indexes might be used as the principal finding aid deserves discussion. There are certainly cases where indexes can refer directly to the original archive, and so may be regarded as the principal finding aids to that entity, rather than as a retrieval aid in support of a textual description. There seem to be three main instances:

(a) If there is an original index, which was compiled and in use during the records' currency, this index (although itself archival) becomes a useful means of access.

(b)   Sometimes an index, rather than a description, may be the most natural finding aid. The example given by Bell[5] is that of the Cabinet Papers from 1938. A structural list for this series can be based upon the administrative history of the cabinet office, plus a note of the chronological sequence of meetings. Since many subjects would be raised at any meeting, the chronological list is not a useful finding aid except to those whose search is narrowly chronological. A subject index to matters considered at each meeting is needed, and is, in effect, the main finding aid for most users. There are other comparable cases: for example, where items in a class are arranged (whether in the original system or not) on alphabetical or numerical references, as with a sequence of case files. Wills are a good example of this type, and these are held by many record offices. Some of these sequences could also be regarded as being self-indexing.

(c)   Some larger repositories based in libraries have the custom of indexing collections of private letters, the index referring directly to the original, and not being derived from, or referring to, terms which appear in the textual description.[6] Since it is possible to write abstracts of letters, or to incorporate names into summary descriptions, this method of operation is based on the design of the finding aid in that repository, and not on the character of the original.

Index planning

Most archivists have some practical familiarity with making indexes, and with the difficulties that come with them. Although most of the older indexes in use today have derived from *ad hoc* and relatively unplanned initiatives, there would be general assent to the proposition that index planning is desirable. An unplanned and undisciplined index is only useful until a certain size and/or degree of congestion is reached. After that, radical reform, including reform of the language used, is needed. In fact, planned decisions are needed on other points as well.

There is, for instance, the question of the underlying structure of the index — is it to be an alphabetised list of terms chosen freely from the natural language (but containing cross-references) or is there to be some control over the terms and concepts to be included in it? If the latter, then is the index to be an application of a general classification scheme, or, as an alternative, is it necessary to compile a special scheme for it?

Indexes arranged under keywords taken from natural language are alphabetic, and those arranged in accordance with a classification scheme are systematic. There is a considerable debate among archivists as to the desirability of each, and it appears that the profession is fairly evenly divided on the question. Most archivists' opinions are formed by what their own experience has been.

The Society of Archivists appointed a working party to construct a general classification scheme for subject indexing. This body met during the latter half of the 1970s. The result was a classification of knowledge structured on an alphanumeric notation. Copies of the first working draft were produced, and put into use experimentally in several archives services and in at least one archive training school. A fully revised draft never appeared, and the scheme was dropped by tacit consent after this degree of experimental use. It is true that some of the opposition to it was not well founded; but archivists found that an elaborate general classification of knowledge, based upon a heavy and inflexible system of notation, did not suit them. There is a high proportion of specialist repositories among archives services, and of course specialist services need specialist classification schemes. More generally, there was no widely felt sense that existing indexes should be recast upon a more structured model, or that there should be a national scheme.

Another classification scheme was produced by the National Register of Archives in 1969, the *Subject Index Scheme and Wordlist.*[7] This was published and made widely available among archives services, and has been updated and revised within the NRA since then. Nevertheless it has never been an important tool in actual indexing practice, and at the present time there is no formally published version available. Like the larger scheme, it has, from the point of view of general use, been withdrawn. Since this scheme did not have

143

the main perceived drawbacks of the larger one, its failure must have derived from more fundamental defects, and in particular, the impossibility of basing archival finding aids on schemes which attempt to classify all knowledge.

> . . . in library catalogues general ideas not only govern the layout of the classification but provide pegs on which to hang references to general works, including the most general of all, such as encyclopaedias. There are no general records in this sense.[8]

All logically structured indexing schemes share the same defect, which is that the indexer has to work with a copy of the scheme on the desk, and has to check each term that has not become familiar. If the scheme is a notational one, the notation has to be learnt and entered, and can often look very odd:

QiNbmGkD29 —
  Buildings
  Planning
    Teacher training college libraries
    Cardiff College of Education

This is an entry from the Classification Research Group's scheme, as used by LISA.[9]

While it is true that indexers can quickly learn the meaning of most of the principal notational codes, nevertheless to use them would still require constant reference to the book, users would need instruction, and there is often a rather cumbersome appearance in the final result.

The criticism mentioned above assumes that a scheme is available in a finished form to start with, which at present is not often the case. It is worth considering whether one of the specialist schemes, such as CRG[10] or SHIC[11] can be adapted for use in an archives office. Even if a suitable scheme is available, there may still be a need to provide for new terms to be included as the work of indexing proceeds. This is a bigger difficulty than it sounds, since new terms have to be slotted into the correct place in the hierarchy, and the correct related terms, at higher and lower levels, must be in place to receive them. Many terms have more than one possible place in the scheme, because they have more than one facet. The operation requires knowledge and judgement, and also consumes time. One cannot expect indexing work to be completed on schedule if the indexer has got to break off constantly to amend the scheme. There is always the diffi-

144

culty of lack of consistency when more than one worker is involved at any stage. This kind of difficulty has certainly caused many indexing schemes to fail, and in doing so has brought their designers into the natural language school of thought.[12]

But then, natural language indexing has also serious problems. The main one is that of synonyms and near synonyms, and behind these lie the array of syntactical and semantic problems which the logical classification schemes attempt to solve.

The indexer has two choices: either to accept any word as a possible entry in the index, no matter what synonyms exist, or to adopt a system of 'preferred terms', and list these in a set of instructions. Both courses have difficulties. The former introduces endless complications into the index, which if continued unchecked will eventually make it difficult to use.

In an uncontrolled natural language index, concepts that are related logically but unrelated alphabetically are randomly scattered. References to an important theme will be divided through all the terms encountered. Bridge construction may be such a theme in county records. The index terms within it might cover planning, procurement, legal provision, transport of materials, the actual building process, maintenance, use by passengers, and so on. Even terms relating to a single level and a specific activity may be scattered: stonework, mortar, bonding, etc. A systematic scheme would be able to bring these together in a logical sequence, and would also direct the mind of the user to new divisions of the scheme which might otherwise have been disregarded. The more specialised the archives on which the index is based the more complex these problems become.

The second course is also difficult. The list of preferred terms, simple enough at first, soon grows to look like a systematic classification scheme, but without the worked-out hierarchical analysis that the latter has. The need to enter preferred terms and cross-references to their alternatives at all the appropriate places means that instructions to the working indexers must get increasingly elaborate, and so must the checking process.

The biggest problem in indexing is probably that of maintaining consistency. So many variations in style, choice of terms, the modification of terms, depth of indexing, etc., are available, that even when the index is the work of only one member of staff over a period (the best way), inconsistencies come in. Classification schemes can certainly be a help, and are sometimes perhaps even indispensable, in combating inconsistency. The golden rule is that any scheme which is adopted should be adopted for the benefit of the user, not directly for that of the indexer.[13]

Where the archives service is territorial, vocabulary control should certainly be supplemented by authority lists of place names. The same choice, between systematic and alphabetical orders, exists here too. Territorial groupings can be preserved by determining a hierarchical order of names, for instance based upon ancient parishes, and within these, townships and other areas of decreasing size. In view of the difficulty of spelling variants over long periods of time, this choice would be a sensible one for a county record office. Rules as to the use of standard spellings and transcribed spellings might appear in the staff instructions: in the index the standard spelling should normally be used.[14]

Personal names do not lend themselves to authority lists in the same way, but they can be subjected to a set of rules about the way they are to be used. Suitable rules appear in several specialist publications as well as in AACR2.[15]

Index planning: procedure

Some mechanical aspects of index construction are also worth thinking about.

Whatever mode of indexing structure is adopted, there must be a decision on the method of alphabetisation, whether 'letter by letter' or 'word by word'. In some cases, this choice can have important consequences.

The choice of typefaces is important. In the past, indexers have had a tendency to insist on using a large number of type variants: capitals, lower case, italic, etc., each style representing some feature inherent in the term used for it. The fullest instance of this is perhaps the index to manuscripts in the British Library.[16] Theoretically, this is a device to bring another channel into use: the type character gives information to the user about certain qualities in the term. Thus, in a personal name index, honorific titles might be given in italic. Elsewhere, capitalised words might indicate those which are included at a certain hierarchical level in the classification scheme.

The index planner must decide whether in fact it is

necessary to include this extra channel. Is it important to the user that this type of information should be given in the main alphabetical sequence? If the information is important, then perhaps a separate place could be found for it. More important than this nowadays is a decision as to whether the cost and difficulty of using a variety of types in one piece of print is justified. The practice is a hangover from a period in which the time of a jobbing printer was cheap. In modern systems, the printer's time is far from cheap, and most word processing systems have little scope for quick changes of typeface. The practice is not generally recommended.

Search requirments

Thinking about how a user's requirements might fit with the special character of the material being indexed, brings one to consider the nature of the terms to be put into the index. Most user enquiries are for subject information which can only be expressed by combining keywords or by using syntactical links between keywords. Neither the requirements of the user nor the concepts contained within documents are likely to be simple. Looked at from either point of view, a typical subject statement might consist of three elements, linked by connecting words.

'(Out-relief) of (agricultural workers) by (Poor Law unions)'

might be an example: the brackets indicate a compound term.

This statement may be made into an entry in a preco-ordinate index by simply writing it out together with the appropriate reference. It can then be rotated, or permuted, by bringing each of the main terms in it to the front:

Agricultural workers, out-relief of by Poor Law unions(ref)
Out-relief of agricultural workers by Poor Law unions.(ref)
Poor Law unions, out-relief of agricultural workers by.(ref)

Such an index is called preco-ordinate because complex statements are co-ordinated before any search is made by the user: each entry consists of a statement which brings together a number of elements to create a complex but precise subject heading. The user's problem with such an index is to identify the heading combinations which will identify the entry required.

The example illustrates that rotating the terms increases

the number of entry points, and makes the problem of identifying correct headings simpler (at the expense of multiplying entries). Even so, it is clear that not every substantive term appears as a heading in the three entries. Some means of access is still needed to:

'relief' (as a term in Poor Law administration),
workers, agricultural,
unions (as units of administration in the Poor Law).

There are also possible synonyms, such as 'poor relief', 'farm workers' or 'boards of guardians' (and many others). These may be covered by a previously determined vocabulary, or by cross-references.

Another approach would be to make the index a postcoordinate one, in which the headings represent only one concept (linked to a reference). Co-ordination of these concepts is then done by the user during the course of a search. The example would read as follows:

Agricultural workers . . . . (ref)
Out-relief. . . . . (ref)
Poor Law unions . . . . (ref)

The problem of synonyms, as before, can be dealt with by vocabulary control, or by cross-references.

In this index, the user must find a way of combining these terms so as to identify the subject statement that is being searched for. The main problem can be seen from the example: the concepts which are used as headings are unqualified, and one cannot see their precise use in the context except by retrieving the documents they refer to. Combining the headings may make a search more precise (thus in the present example, it is possible that only one reference may have entries for all three terms), which perhaps makes this type of index better for mechanised systems.

All three headings in the example are terms which occur at different levels in a classification scheme, and are also terms which have more than one facet.

Agriculture	Population	Primary production
Labour	Rural population	Agricultural prdn
Farm workers	Farm workers	Labour

Employment	Poor Law
Wages	Unions
Agricultural wages	Relief
Supplementation	Out-relief etc.
Out-relief	

The illustration suggests the possibility of an alternative form of index, the chain. In this system, all the relevant terms at different hierarchical levels are displayed in turn, in such a way that the terms at levels below the one being used as a heading are given. In the example, possible chain entries would be these:

Poor Law. Unions. Relief. Out-relief
Unions. Relief. Out-relief
Relief. Out-relief
Out-relief

When sorted alphabetically this would become:

Out-relief. . . . . (ref)
Poor Law. Unions. Relief. Out-relief . . . . (ref)
Relief. Out-relief. . . . . (ref)
Unions. Relief. Out-relief . . . . (ref)

The principle is that terms below the lead terms in hierarchical level are all repeated, but not those above it. It is still necessary to use vocabulary control to deal with the problem of synonyms.

It will be noticed that the chain index is a preco-ordinated index, so that it will be judged by its ability to bring together linked concepts in a useful way. It also needs a classification scheme which provides the necessary hierarchy of terms. The East Sussex Record Office experimented with chain indexing in the 1970s but the experiment was not successful.[17] The lack of a previously established classification scheme meant that staff had to invent linkages, or replicate terms uselessly. In an archival context, the system is likely to interest only specialist archives services which cover technical fields and have written a suitable classification scheme.

Any index can be considered for automation, and any automated system of description will make provision for an indexing component.

A basic distinction is between systems in which the index headings are selected by the computer (machine-generated indexes), and those in which the terms are selected by the staff and the computer is used to arrange and display them. These two methods may sometimes be combined to some extent.

Not much space need be given to considering human-generated indexes, for here the computer does not introduce an essentially new feature. It is merely a device for reducing the clerical work involved in organising the index entries once they have been written. Even so, the efficiency and speed with which this is done may well make the difference between success or failure of an indexing scheme, especially when considered from a budgetary point of view.

Human-generated indexes may operate in one of two ways. In the first, the indexer scans the textual descriptions and marks in tags which will instruct the system to extract the tagged terms as index headings. It is possible to use different tags so that the system can differentiate between different indexes (place, persons, subject), or between headings, qualifiers and linking terms.

The example shown is from a page of listing for a large manuscript library:[18]

'Throughout please divide text as follows: 2MS no.2 3BIB.REF.3 4incipit4 5ends5 6other title6 7language7 8keyword8 9authentication9 10date10.'

In the second way, the indexer may extract the terms to be used in the index, and write them separately into an input field. This was done in the PROSPEC-SA experiment, and a box was provided for index keywords in the input document. It might be thought that this method demands an unjustifiable input of skilled labour. Certainly it must be a relatively expensive method, since it involves rewriting some of the material. On the other hand, this is an approach which gives the maximum amount of control over the generation of the index, which in turn means that there is less likelihood of the index becoming choked with useless or unintelligible entries.

It may be advisable where the index is a complex one, carried out at some depth on important documents.

Whichever method is used for selecting terms, there still remain problems in automating their retrieval and setting them out in a usable index. There are several systems which could be used.

The automated indexing system known as PRECIS has been used since 1971 to index the bibliographic descriptions in the British National Bibliography, and it is therefore an established system which would in certain circumstances be available for adoption by other information services. It provides a permuted preco-ordinate index which takes account of syntactical relationships.

> PRECIS . . . has been used also by a number of other institutions and has proved acceptable to them as a method of producing a subject index to a classified arrangement of citations and as an economically viable method of producing such an index. Once the subject statements have been written and organised according to the rules of the system, the remainder of the index production can be carried out entirely by machine manipulation of the data.[19]

PRECIS provides a clearly readable layout:

Lead term   Qualifier
  Display

Entries describing the assessment of student-archivists on courses at universities might appear thus:

1. Universities
   Archive schools. Students. Assessment.

2. Archives schools. Universities.
   Students. Assessment.

3. Students. Archives schools. Universities.
   Assessment.

4. Assessment. Students. Archives schools. Universities.

PRECIS is quoted as a sophisticated subject indexing system which would appear to have considerable potential for use with archives, and which would require some method of human selection for the index headings.

The next stage of automation would logically be one where the system itself could identify the keywords and qualifiers to be used as index entries. So far, however, no system for this has managed to avoid serious difficulties.

The great advantage of machine-generated indexing systems is, of course, that the computer takes out most of the labour costs of selecting and setting out the headings, and all of the labour involved in arranging and displaying them. The main defect is that mindless operations involved in displaying strings of characters may often result in meaningless entries.

One of the most successful formats for a machine-generated index is that of the KWIC (keyword in context) index. This is particularly suitable for indexing one-line dossier titles, and so would seem to be especially useful for RM and for item-level descriptions. The system reproduces the whole of a line of text, permuting it about each word in the line. Stop lists can be used to prevent linking words such as 'the', 'of', etc. from appearing in the index. The index line runs down the centre of the page (see Figure 13).

An alternative layout is KWOC (keyword out of context) in which each word in the line is taken in turn (excluding words in the stop list) and printed in the left margin. The line is then repeated below it, together with the reference. The difference between KWIC and KWOC is essentially one of output layout, not of term selection. Both therefore suffer from the same limitation, that the immediate context of the keyword must be sufficient to explain its meaning.

These indexing systems naturally generate very long indexes, and also, when being run, take a good deal of memory space within the computer. They do provide an entirely automatic index, which does not attempt any degree of syntactical or semantic analysis, but which does achieve at least some degree of preco-ordination of terms.

Automatic indexing systems such as these are provided as part of several information or text management packages, and are often readily available without special programming. They can also be used to provide concordances (lists of terms, with or without a count of the number of times each is used) to texts, which in turn can be an essential tool in composing classification schemes or thesauri. A number of computer packages can also incorporate and apply locally constructed thesauri.

All computerised indexes, whether machine-generated or not, can be formatted to provide output in convenient ways. The ESRO experience is useful again here: their system

(a) KWIC

```
1          FOREIGN OFFICE DOCUMENTS

6          Agreement, Commerce, etc (Basutoland, Bechuanaland and Swaziland and Mozambique).

1                                    King Hussein and his sons, Vol.IV,
4                                    King Hussein; interviews with, etc, regarding his future status,

2 tared and treasures removed from the Prophet's tomb at Medina.

9 tension of Extradition Treaty of 1911 -        to Zanzibar and -        British Solomon Islands,
5 ate (including the Mainland Dominions of the Sultan of Zanzibar); question of subsequent re-entry into the diplomat:
```

(b) KWOC

Basutoland

```
   1930   Feb 13,18.   FO93/77.   100.   Agreement, Commerce, etc
          (Basutoland, Bechuanaland and Swaziland and Mozambique).
```

Bechuanaland

```
   1930   Feb 13,18.   FO93/77.   100.   Agreement, Commerce, etc
          (Basutoland, Bechuanaland and Swaziland and Mozambique).
```

Burma.

```
   1937 Mar 31.  FO93/95.  37.  Notes on nationality of persons
        affected by re-delimitation of boundary between Tenasserim
        and Siam.
```

Figure 13 KWIC and KWOC indexes
[Based on Public Record Office, *Lists & Indexes*, Supplementary Series XIII, 12]
Source: University of Liverpool

153

provided for the computer to print out index entries on cards, which could easily be duplicated for cross-referencing, and which could be inserted alphabetically in the existing file. This operation proved wasteful, since computers are well able to print out updated indexes at convenient intervals, and can also combine two or more indexes provided that they are held in structurally compatible files. In most cases they can also be searched, so that the printout index is not necessarily the most useful format for the resulting work.

Interactive searching

Bartle and Cook's survey in 1982 found that in every case where an automated system had been adopted for archival description, the output was designed to be assimilated to traditional hard-copy formats. Computers were being used as tools to produce the same kind of finding aids as had been produced by manual methods in the past.[20]

The reasons for this apparently excessive conservatism were to be found both in the limitations of the computer systems available to archivists up to the early 1980s, and in the situation of most archive services at that time.

At the time of the survey, only a handful of archives services had managed to get access to interactive systems, and probably not more than two or three had on-line terminals within the repository. The PRO had successfully run an interactive system for the control of document movements within the building.[21] Elsewhere, interactive systems were restricted to cases where the archives service was responsible for current record systems or documentation services, or was closely linked with these. This meant that other archives services were limited to batch mode systems, which naturally implied that the output most easily used and controlled took the form of printout, or, in some cases, of formally published catalogues.

In this context, archives services saw their best policy as being one of continuing existing series of finding aids (particularly where these took the form of published volumes). The largest of these services outside the PRO, the Department of Manuscripts of the British Library, explicitly took this view. Their policy was to use computing services to reduce the burden of clerical and other routine work involved in the production of their published catalogues.[22] Other major repositories, such as the Greater London Record Office, took a similar view. In other cases the computer was used to introduce a new type of finding aid — for instance the West Sussex Record Office's index to wills — but here too the emphasis was on the production of updatable hard copy formats.

However by the early 1980s it became clear that computers would be available cheaply for interactive facilities, especially the storage and searching of data bases, and from this point it has become necessary for archivists to include this possibility in their planning for retrieval strategies in the future. The first voice to be raised to this effect was D. Bearman's in the USA, who met with considerable resistance.[23] Since then the spread of micro-computers has rendered his view less unfashionable. Some description of the procedures and difficulties of interactive searching is therefore necessary here.

It is of course possible to use a computer to search a data base held within its memory, even if interactive facilities are not available. This would involve the user in framing a question, the answer to which would be the information required (assuming that this information was thought to be held in the data base). The trouble is that, for reasons discussed in the earlier part of this chapter, it is not easy to formulate a complex question, using exactly the right keywords and linked combinations of keywords, so that they match exactly the index headings held in the system (or strings of characters in the text). Usually it is necessary to make several attempts, modifying the terms used in the light of results obtained. This means that offline access to the computer is frustrating, and retrieval by this means is likely to be inaccurate and slow.

Interactive facilities, in which the user can directly question the computer and get an immediate answer, transform this situation. The user can now ask for the retrieval of data on documents which contain his specified keywords. The reply may suggest that a different keyword or combination of keywords should be tried: this can be done, and another answer received. The process of question and answer can be carried on, the questions becoming more and more refined each time, until the user can be satisfied that all relevant information has been retrieved. The final version can then, if required, be printed out.

If any data base can be searched in this way, it is easy to

see that the index format may well have become redundant, for the computer can just as easily search for specified terms within the body of a piece of text, as in an alphabetically arranged list of headings. The only requirement is that the original programming, or software package, provides the facility for this kind of search. All that is required is that the user should be able to identify a set of keywords, and the logical connections between them, which the machine can use as the keys to its search.

Early computer systems had the drawback that keywords entered for a search had to be exactly matched in the text. Capital letters or plural terminations, for example, might cause a search to fail. Modern systems do not usually suffer from this defect, as they allow the user to override capitals or lower-case differences, and to specify alternative terminations (or prefixes) to words. Thus the search term 'train+' could produce a response to 'trains' and 'training' as well as to the string specified. More sophisticated ways of linking terms which are related linguistically but which differ in some way from each other (lemmatisation) also exist but are probably not especially relevant to archival management.

Computer systems which provide searching facilities usually require that the user should be able to use a command language, which consists of a sequence of commands chosen from a permitted range, and which cause the system to work in the required way. Command languages vary a great deal in complexity. Some are quite simple and knowledge of these can easily be acquired by users. More complex command languages need more study, and these would be better used by trained staff. Naturally, the more complex the language, the more elaborate the search procedures that are possible. This may be a limiting factor, especially if the searching is to be done by external users or relatively inexpert people.

It is possible to overcome the problem in some cases by undertaking extra programming, and adding a 'front-end' system to the programmes being used. This system might prompt the user by writing out a sequence of plain-language questions to which an answer is required. A sequence of question and answer might be as follows:

User:	'Search'
Computer:	What is the name of the data base you wish to search?
User:	'Strangford papers'
Computer:	OK. What is the first keyword?

Special programming of this sort can often make a complex system more user-friendly, but it does also have drawbacks. Users rapidly become expert in the system they have learnt. When this happens they become impatient with the constant repetition of prompts, and it may be useful to introduce an optional choice of level, which allows the expert user to switch off prompts which have become too elementary.

Keywords to be searched for may be linked by logical operators, based upon Boolean algebra. For most purposes there are three of these: AND, OR and NOT.

Fish AND chips	instructs the system to find every instance in which a record contains both terms.
Fish OR chips	finds every record in which one of the terms occurs.
Fish NOT chips	finds records in which one of the terms appears but leaves out those in which they both appear together.

The logical operators can be used to link three or more terms in any combination:

Fish AND chips NOT newspapers.
Fish OR chips OR cartons.

Keywords may also be combined into single compound terms, and two or more of these compound terms can also be combined in a search:

(Fish AND chips) AND (paper OR wrapping) NOT cartons.

As far as the mechanism of searching is concerned, these command facilities are flexible and intelligible, and allow a very wide range of search enquiries to be made. Difficulties experienced in carrying out a search usually derive far more from the difficulties inherent in formulating a search request than from the difficulties of interpreting it for the computer.

These difficulties, however, are considerable. The problem is to match the descriptions of archival entities which have been put into the data base with the ideas formulated by users. If this match is to be made, there must be compatibility between the terminology (and even between the habits of thought and background knowledge) used by the archivist and by the user. This is asking a lot even if one could assume that most users could formulate their enquiries in clear terms. Most often users need the stimulus of contact with the material before they can devise meaningful keywords for a retrieval strategy: browsing may be the best introduction for them.

There are many possibilities of failure. The user may not succeed in thinking of and then asking for the keywords which are present in the data base (a synonym may have been used); the system may not have recognised the keyword asked for (some difference in format may not have been discounted); or the keyword combinations asked for may produce a flood of positive replies which take great labour to distinguish from each other. There may be too few hits, or too many. The possibilities of refinement of searches which are inherent in interactive searching may reduce this hiatus between the system and the user, but it is a gap which is always likely to exist. Even more is the gap between the thought and language of the archivist who originally devised the description which is being searched and those of the users of it. Ultimately it is a question of bridging the gap between minds. In some respects computers have reduced this gap, because they can sometimes minimise the labour involved in checking possibilities. In other ways, though, it is possible that they have increased the gap, because they tend to shield their holdings behind technological screens.

Automatic data processing in archival management

Information management today cannot be carried on without consideration of the use of computers, which are machines for the storage, processing and transfer of information. The ready availability and growing storage capacity of microcomputers, and the general introduction of on-line multi-terminal systems in administration mean that computing services of some kind are within the reach of most administrative or research departments, however small and isolated they may be. Archives services are not excluded from this generality, even though at the time of writing, the majority of established archives services are still being run manually.[1]

There have been four surveys of computer applications in archives, applicable to Britain, and these have charted the rather unsteady progress of new automated systems in this field. The first, edited by L. Bell and M. Roper[2] was the report of an international seminar held in 1974. Most of the participants represented major national archives institutions – Britain, Canada, USA, Belgium, France, West Germany, Italy, the Netherlands, and USSR. There was only one contribution from a local archives service. This was the East Sussex Record Office (ESRO) which has the distinction of being the first non-national record office to undertake major automation.

The second survey was by L. Bell in 1975, and was the report of an enquiry into current systems in use in Britain: at that time it appears that there were some fifteen active archival computer applications. However six of these were within the PRO and five of them might properly be categorised as programs for aspects of historical research. Many of the systems noted were for the production of indexes.[3]

Cook's survey published in 1980 was partial, but broke new ground in noting the arrival of automated systems in records management. It was still assumed at this date that most archival automation was occurring in the big national archives institutions, libraries and museums.[4]

Finally, R. Bartle and M. Cook carried out a more detailed survey of computer applications in Britain, outside the PRO, in the latter half of 1982. This found that there had been considerable new work, and that new developments were coming to light very rapidly. Seven organisations (including four county record offices) were operating automated systems for RM; eighteen were developing them for archival management; and there were a few other cases of specific applications such as the indexing of particular classes. A feature of this report was that a majority of systems noted had been introduced since 1980, and that interactive and microcomputer schemes were beginning to predominate.[5]

It would be wrong to give the impression that this series of surveys shows an uninterrupted progress in computer development. On the contrary, the course of development had been patchy and prone to setbacks. Some of the systems introduced with high expectations in the 1970s have failed entirely: this includes the first local record office scheme, ESRO, which has now been withdrawn. Some have been substantially curtailed as a result of difficulties encountered: this includes the PRO's main system, PROSPEC. Proposals for networking or co-operative action have either been abortive (PROSPEC-SA), or are conspicuous by their absence. It is clearly true that the early computer applications have nearly all suffered severe setbacks as a result of software design defects or the logistical and administrative difficulties of communicating with the computing services. New computer applications have only appeared after new software has become available, and after the appearance of computing facilities much nearer to the user than the old ones were. There is little future for batch mode working in the archival context; but interactive working, with an on-site terminal or microcomputer, is developing fast.

There has so far been no serious attempt in Britain to create a central on-line data base of archival information, comparable to any of the bibliographic or documentary data bases. In North America, the RLIN network is now operational, so that it is clear that this lack is not the result of some inherent impossibility.[6] On the other hand, archives services generally hold bulky materials which have a low reference rate. Much of the expected realisable value of archival information resides in their use in the remote future. Perhaps it will always be difficult to justify the use of data base systems whose main virtue is rapid retrieval.

The archive services of highly specialised institutions are perhaps to be regarded as exceptions to this: the BBC Written

160

Archives, hospital medical records services, and the archives of research institutes in the natural sciences, are possible examples. Outside these kinds of institutions, rapidity of retrieval of information ranks lower than does accurate and full retrieval. One may conclude that computer systems, in an archival context, are best used to manage the materials within the service, by controlling management processes, and by facilitating the production of finding aids.

Archival description

Computerising archival description is a much more complicated process than computerising the description of books. There has been no generally accepted standard of description; whether the publication of MAD in 1985 has changed this still remains to be seen. The problem of description at several levels, each of which has its own descriptive character, makes it difficult to devise record formats which will suit the realities of archives administration. There has been insufficient preparatory work on the problems of indexing or searching free text descriptive entries. In addition, there have been problems of staff retraining, or of the hostility of some existing personnel, and there have been problems of access to computing services.

Data capture. The first difficulty in introducing automated description systems is how to assemble the data which is to be written into the descriptions. This problem of course exists in non-automated systems also. Bartle and Cook noted that archives services have rarely sought to alter their existing administrative arrangements: the thinking was that computers could perhaps be used to streamline existing processes, but should not seriously influence the methods of work of professional staff, or the way duties might be delegated within the office. The British Library feasibility study made a specific commitment to this principle.[7] The PRO's data capture procedures for PROSPEC assume that the computer has made virtually no alteration to the previously existing delegation of duties.[8]

The conservatism which is evidenced in staffing structures and procedures is based on the view that data capture is a matter of filling in paper forms, which are adaptations from, and represent, traditional listing stationery. Where batch mode working is the norm, this is not surprising. Record

161

MODERN RECORDS CENTRE - FILE DETAILS

N = NEW COMPUTER RECORDS

| RECORDS CENTRE NUMBER | DEPT/SECTION | DEPARTMENTAL FILE REFERENCE | FORM A or B | LOCATION | | | | | FILE DATE | | ACTION | | NAME OF FILE |
				Serial	Box	Rack	Bay	Shelf	From	To	Date Mon. Yr	Mark	

Figure 14 Data input form, Berkshire Record Office

Source: Bartle and Cook, p. 18

offices have designed input data forms which are versions of their usual lists. The Berkshire RM input form, is a direct adaptation of the previously used transfer list, the main difference in which is that spaces for individual characters are provided, in order to control field length[9] (see Figure 14).

Data input forms are designed in the light of the office procedures they are to be a part of, and in the light of the methods by which the data is to be processed. Usually this has been by keyboarding the data remotely, so that clarity of instructions to the operator is an important feature. The other main features are

(a)   the description is broken up as far as possible into clearly defined fields, the contents of which are restricted in length and character; and

(b)   as far as possible the work processes are reduced to a sequence of narrow choices. These points may be illustrated in turn.

A reasonably strictly controlled input data form is that of PROSPEC, which allows a variable-length free text description in its central fields, but provides tight control of the peripheral fields. For example, entries in the 'date' field are limited to those which conform to a list of possibilities set out in the system manual. The range of possibilities allowed demonstrates the difficulty archivists have in establishing definite descriptive usages: the range of information and format in archives is too great. The purpose of this kind of field limitation is to reduce the possibilities of error where the data processing is to be carried out by inexpert clerical staff at a distance.[10]   The example shown is from the PROSPEC-SA adaptation (see Figure 15).

The cataloguing cards in use at the British Antarctic Survey (see Figure 16), which are based upon the cards designed by the Museum Documentation Association, were designed in 1981–2, and demonstrate clearly that there has been a great improvement in the flexibility of field structures allowed within computer files. On the cards the item descriptions are divided into single-field boxes. It is assumed that some fields (for example the location code) will contain only a short entry, consisting of an alphanumeric reference code; but this assumption is not backed by automatic restriction. There is a good deal of free text: the main function of the field boxes is to ensure that all relevant details are entered (fields can be left empty if necessary), and to allow the possibility of

PROSPEC-SA DATA FORM 1A

Record Office

Batch Code	nbatch	
Record Office and Class Code	00	
Number of pieces	02	
First Date	03	
Last Date	04	
Physical Nature	05	
Title	06	
Description	07	
Index Terms	08	
Local Code	13	
Manipulation Codes	14	
Source	15 end end batch	

Figure 15   Data input form, PROSPEC-SA
Source: PROSPEC entry form

164

sorting the data on any particular field. The relative flexibility of this data entry system also assumes that the data processing can be done in-house, or at least near at hand to the staff actually working on the records.[11]

The second point may be illustrated by the input form from St. John's College, Cambridge[12] (see Figure 17).

The top half of this form consists of multiple-choice questions. The archivist completes the form by simply checking the choices, and the data processor keys a single letter. This simplifies and codifies the work processes at both levels. The free text description at the bottom provides facilities for tagging index keywords.[13]

Finally the data input forms proposed for some large manuscript libraries are designed to allow the maximum of unstructured text. The boxes and other divisions on the paper merely give indications that certain types of information should be provided, and give space for them. Tagging controls the use of different typefaces in the output, to provide a catalogue which is uniform with the manually produced catalogues of previous years. Since the data is not strongly structured into fields, it is not visualised that sorting the material into output arranged under a variety of field headings will be needed. The objective here is simply to produce a traditional catalogue, but with computer assistance in the processing.[14]

An important problem for archives staffs in connection with data input, is to find a way which is perceived as clear and natural for both archivists and the clerical staff of the archives service. It is desirable for the success of the system that data input and processing should be done as close to the site of the professional work as possible. Physical remoteness of data processing services has been an important factor in the failure of some systems in the past, and a cause of staff hostility.

In the past, there have been two ways of bringing description and processing closer together. One way is to use purpose-designed input hardware, such as the Direct Data Entry machines which were chosen by the Dyfed Record Office. These are essentially keyboards which write the input data electronically on to tape cassettes. Program information can be encoded on a control tape, which then provides prompts (questions which the typist has to answer) and also controls the validity of the data entered (only numerical data can be entered in a numbers field, etc.). This type of equipment is now largely being superseded by visual display units,

Card of	Institution			Archive Code		1
	N.E.R.C.: BRITISH ANTARCTIC SURVEY			AD6/2E/1947/K1		

PROVENANCE	Division		Section		Record Identity	
					76/48 & K21/1947/E	
	Author/s				Place	
	Tonkin, J.E.				E	
	Date/s (c) April 1947					

	Record Type	Title	
	Internal report	Sledging journey March – April 1947	

Contents

SUBJECT DESCRIPTION

Site: "Soda Slope" (now North east Glacier) &   Armadillo Hill
Date: 2 March 1947 = 13 April 1947
Persons: Mason, D.P. & Walton, E.W.K. & Butson, A.R.C. &   (author)
Activity: Travel reconnaissance & survey
Place: Fallieres Coast &   Bowman Coast
Coords: SR19-20/2 & SR19-20/3

BAS G1	GENERAL INDEX CARD	Edition 2	August 1981	Printed by NERC, Reprographic Services	C

REFERENCES

Associated
Documents

Publications   reference only/quotation   in part/complete   altered/unaltered

Author: date: title: journal/publisher: vol: details

CONSERVATION

Physical format

Copy 1 (new cover); 11 pp (paginated)

Condition

Conservator   To   From

Work done

MANAGEMENT

Transfer to Archives	Accession & Process Record	Access Code
Location	Record Transfer List	Disposal Code

INDEX

(Additional to contents)	Particular
General Cross ref.	

Figure 16   BAS cataloguing cards
Source: Bartle and Cook, p. 22

166

Sequence no.	*N **1791**		Refer to	*R 1789
Piece no(s)	*I 36·158		+of+ 36·141 - 36·165	
Class(es)	*C DER			

Location (one only)	*W Ⓜ Mun. Room	Material (one or two)	*M P paper
	L Library		Ⓡ parchment
	T Treasury		O other
	G Lodge		
	C Chapel Office	State (one only)	*S D damaged
	V Vestry		I incomplete
	C College Office		Ⓖ good
	S Sen. Tutor		O other
	O other		
		Language(s) *G Ⓔ English	
Form (one only)	*F V vol or sewn	(one or two)	L Latin
	Ⓛ loose		F French
	R roll		O other
	F file		
	G guarded	Authent. (one or two)	*A N none
	M map or plan		Ⓢ signed
	O other		Ⓦ sealed
			O other
Decoration (one only)	*H D decorated		
	Ⓝ not decorated		

Date(s)

| 1 | 4 | 8 | 0 | | | 0 | 4 | | | 2 | 6 | | | | | | | | | | | | | |

< year > .? <month> .? < day > c? -s < year > .? <month> .? < day > c?

? doubtful   c approximate   s scattered

Accession

¬ Acc

< year > .? <month> .? < day > c?

Keyword(s)   Precede names and places by #

                  Precede other keywords by ¬

Domestic arrangement between Miles Wandesford of Thriplow
& Katherine Harley of London widow
# Cs + Thriplow   # Wandesford. Miles   # Harley. Katherine

¬ Domestic. arrangement

Supplementary information on
reverse.

Figure 17   Completed input form, St. John's College, Cambridge

Source: Bartle and Cook, p. 48

so that the second method of interfacing is now becoming more common.

What is required for this is front-end programming, so that the input of data into a system is governed by a subordinate program. This will probably set up a formatted screen: labelled spaces will appear on the VDU screen, corresponding to the fields into which data is to be entered. Alternatively, a series of prompts can be supplied, and the operator will have to provide data in answer to these. Without such user-friendly devices, it can be difficult to control the entry and checking of data, and on this will depend the success of the whole system.

Most data entry systems assume that the existing relationship between professional staff and clerical staff will persist into the future. Archivists generate text (usually by writing in longhand on paper); typists process this text so that it is legible and reproducible. The potential of mobile multistation computer systems however is so great that senior management of archives services should now be considering whether professional staff should not be retrained to input data directly into the system.

Levels. The analysis of archival arrangement in Chapter 5 showed that the question of levels is an important one. In general archival materials will normally be described at several levels — at least two, and possibly as many as eight or nine. Descriptions at different levels have different characteristics and are treated in different ways. Macro descriptions may be grouped together in horizontal collections, to produce guides. Micro descriptions are less frequently gathered together, but are lengthy and may be assembled as a collection of lists. Most descriptions at all levels, but especially at micro levels, consist of a headnote which is free text, followed by a structured list. Vertically collected descriptions at several levels are published as catalogues.[15]

1. Horizontal collections of macro descriptions.

(a) Guides and handlists.

The group/subgroup descriptions do not in themselves pose much of a problem for automation, since they are relatively homogeneous, and consist mainly of connected narrative. Automated systems could treat these through word processing, much as any text for publication is treated. Indexing can be provided for by tagging, or by a concordance

168

facility in the software. More serious problems arise when class descriptions are added, as they normally are. Class descriptions consist of some free text, but with associated dedicated fields, and present a much more structured picture. They contrast clearly with the higher level descriptions, and it is difficult to conceive a system which will contain both types of data structure within a single processing system.

Faced with this problem, the PRO decided to concentrate their automated system on the class descriptions and to leave the group/subgroup descriptions on a manual basis. This procedure has proved workable, but clearly has disadvantages. The decision was taken at a time when the storage of data within the computer was much more expensive, and subject to more physical limitations, than it is now. Word processing facilities were then less common, and it was not so feasible to use word processors as data entry devices, or as output devices, to and from mainframe computers.

For the production of guides, a system is needed which will allow total freedom in the construction, length and content of fields, and permit the combination of long free text entries, followed by the somewhat more structured sequences of class descriptions. The index should be capable of drawing keywords from both parts. The system should allow retrieval of data by using any of the distinguishable fields as the basis of a sort. This amounts to a complicated and difficult specification, which would probably not be met by any existing commercial software package.

(b) Lists and inventories.

Micro descriptions, being essentially lists, do not present the same difficulties. The increasing flexibility of computer systems have reduced any difficulties there may have been in using variable length and free text fields, so that considerable variations in, for example, the length of file titles, can easily be accommodated. Dedicated fields to contain reference codes, dates, and other information can be created or deleted quite easily in many systems.

The headnote which many lists require might perhaps bring in some of the problems experienced in the macro descriptions. In practice, however, several data base systems available now will provide for headnotes and column headings of at least moderate length. This will probably be sufficient for most archivists, especially if an office rule is introduced which will encourage general information on an archival entity to be put into the macro descriptions rather than into a headnote governing a micro description. Indexing should not present any new problem.

2. Vertical descriptions.

When vertical assemblies of descriptions are brought in, complications once again begin to appear. A catalogue of a collection or group, ranging through perhaps four, perhaps six levels, will include so many different description structures that one might be tempted to treat the question as one of text processing. Is a catalogue not to be treated as a kind of publication? Certainly many catalogues have been published, either as bound books, or in some less formal way. The preparation of texts of this kind would be a suitable job for automated publication systems.

Such a suggestion, though certainly feasible, negates the possibility of a central electronic data base for an archival system. Moreover, there are different kinds of finding aid possible, other than guides, lists and catalogues. Handlists of selected types of document; subject guides selected from various parts of the collection; location lists, microform catalogues, lists by date, physical condition, language, possession of seals — these are all examples of the possible output from an archival data base. If this kind of selection and ordering is to be possible, the system must be able to recognise appropriate field labels, index tags and other control symbols, when they occur throughout a range of record structures.

System specification

It is fairly safe to say that no software house has yet produced a system which is capable of solving all these problems. Text management systems are being actively developed, as are searching facilities, and it is possible that archivists may find that they can devise a way of bringing their description systems within the ambit of a loosely controlled free text package. At the moment, however, this prospect looks unlikely. It is more likely that, by changing their own systems of description, archivists may respond to the appearance of systems which give rapid search facilities to long textual entries.

At the present time, pending such radical new developments, it is more practical to consider limited computer systems, which carry out a limited range of tasks within the

170

service. All successful systems of today are of this kind: PROSPEC (which has had several original features truncated); the RM systems; lists and indexes of specific types or collections. Systems which approached the aims of a general data base (such as ARCAIC) are the ones which have not succeeded.

For this reason, computerised methods can be considered for the control of archives of specific types, such as title deeds, maps or letters. There are active systems for all of these.

Two county record offices have systems for listing title deeds, in association with the terrier of county property. Maps are listed with computer aid in several institutions, including some libraries and museums: they are an easy subject for they resemble bibliographic descriptions in the uniformity of their data structure, and have a ready market for sale or distribution of the output; they are also normally described at one level only, the item.

Letters are more complex, for there is no generally accepted standard for their description. The catalogue of Nelson's letters, produced by the National Maritime Museum, might be regarded as an interesting model. Data is structured into dedicated fields, and the resulting data base is used to produce six differently sorted lists: in order of record number, class mark, date, recipient, place of writing (alphabetically), and place of writing by date (this produces an itinerary of Nelson's movements). This imaginative project illustrates the great potential there is even in restricted computer systems, but it must be remembered that since this is a single-level item-by-item list of documents, all problems of multi-level descriptions have been side-stepped.[16]

Packaged systems

Until the development of computer systems which will accommodate a full archival data base, archivists will be interested in the possibilities of existing information management software packages. Several are in use in an archival context, and there is rapid development in this area.

The first need is for a systems analysis which will make clear the aims and objectives of a proposed archival automation, and give a value to the parameters. Formal analyses of this kind have been undertaken by a few archives services, including the PRO and, more recently, by the University of

171

Southampton in connection with its management of the Wellington papers. A summary of this has been published in 1984 by C.M. Philips and C.M. Woolgar, and should serve as a useful guide to similar work by smaller archives services.[17]

The main commercial packages which have been used by archivists for their projects up to the present are FAMULUS, STAIRS, and INSPEC. The Southampton project has adopted STATUS. In addition, several employ versions of the Museum Documentation Association's GOS. The University of Glasgow is in the process of developing a package with specific archival needs in mind, and which is in use there already — this is known as PARCH.

INSPEC is the basis of the PRO's adapted version, PROSPEC. Despite the experimental extension of this package to external archives services, in the form of PROSPEC-SA, this system as it stands (although effective in its present use) is probably not suitable for further adoption. For its first years it used an obsolescent format for data entry (paper tape), and used external bureau services for data processing. These methods have changed, but an external commentator may still find the interface between the archivists and the computer service rather cumbersome. If the proposal for any sort of national network were to be revived, it is probable that a new prospectus would have to be drawn up for it, and this certainly would take account of developments in data base technology which have occurred since the system was designed.

STAIRS is widely available with IBM hardware, which must make it a popular choice for many data processing services. It has an interesting archival application in the House of Lords Record Office, which has used it to construct a list of acts of parliament. At the time of writing this project is suspended for financial reasons, but the input of data had been going on for some time, and the resulting data base had every appearance of being a successful one.[18] There are also some well-established archival projects in Europe and America which use this package.

However a closer look at the STAIRS software and command languages suggests that in its present state it is not suitable for adoption by smaller archives services unless they are prepared to use bureau services for their data preparation. STAIRS is designed to supply the software for a central data base in a large organisation, but it works on the assumption that there is a specialist data processing team in charge of the structure of files and data input. Users who are not DP specialists will find it difficult to manipulate the package, to make it respond to the precise structures and specifications required for a file of archival descriptions. Conducting searches and retrieving information is somewhat easier. File structure and data input can be vastly improved, however, if the user has access to other IBM software, and particularly to their office communication and recording system known as PROFS. This is available both on IBM mainframe computers equipped with interactive terminals and also on the IBM PC microcomputers.

The package which up to now has had the widest use among archives services is FAMULUS. This was one of the earliest text management packages available, and is widely and cheaply available, especially to academic users. There are successful archival applications using it in several places, and it is the software which underlies further programming in several new applications. Unfortunately FAMULUS does have some serious defects. It was designed as a small-scale bibliographic package (the notional equivalent of a 'shoe-box of cards'), and some versions have limits on the number and size of fields. It was designed at a time when data input was normally by way of punched cards, and retains this termin- ology and mentality, even though most users have now adapted it to other forms of input. The 'search' facility in FAMULUS is also limited to certain fields, at least in some versions.

These are important defects, but in the summer of 1984 the Computer Board allocated funds to allow new program- ming to be undertaken, and it is expected that a radically revised version of FAMULUS, written in FORTRAN 77, and designed for interactive use, will be available during 1984/5. If this timetable is held to, this package will remain a serious contender as the leading archival software. FAMULUS has ten programmes, which carry out all the standard procedures needed by archivists: file structure, entry/editing of text, sorting on fields, merging files, construction of indexes (including KWIC), searching and outputting results. Present versions are weak on formatting output.

Glasgow University Archives took a strong initiative during the early 1980s in the design of special software for archival management. They completed an early version of the package they have named PARCH, for which a prospectus has been issued. To the outsider, the original concepts behind PARCH appear to be similar to those of FAMULUS, but several of the difficulties in the latter seem to have been smoothed out. There is to be a microcomputer version. Unfortunately, although GUA has used this software to produce and output material from several data bases, and also for some historical work, the package remains incomplete and so cannot be tested elsewhere. At the time of writing, there is no timetable for its completion.[19]

The Museum Documentation Association's package GOS has several versions and has been in use in museums for some years. The MDA is co-operating with a working party of the Society of Archivists with the object of producing a version suitable for archival management. The possibilities of this were demonstrated in practice at the Society's in-service course in Cambridge in 1982, and are linked with the BAS data input card illustrated above. The capabilities of GOS appear to be considerable, especially since the MDA operates as a supporting bureau service. Microcomputer versions are in preparation. It is true that in some practical respects the software remains dependent on Cambridge computer installations, and in its present version is portable only through landline links, but the MDA consistently state that it is to be made fully portable.[20]

The University of Southampton study has led to a comparison of performance estimates by a number of software houses, and it appears likely that the ICL package STATUS will also in the future be a leading contender. Its chief drawback seems to be that it is available only in the commercial sphere, and is thought to be expensive.

Other computer applications in archives are supported by in-house programming or in-house computer facilities, particularly those of local government. All the established RM systems and some of the archival systems which are operational today in fact depend on the active co-operation and close liaison with the employing organisation's computer. Any archivist wishing to plan for a computer application would be well advised to start by establishing such a connection. The success of a system depends so much on local technical support.

Hardware

Archival management requires relatively little operational complexity from a computer: entry and editing text, sorting,

174

searching, and indexing specified terms. These are relatively simple operations for most modern computer systems, and indeed many of them can usually be provided by the resident operating system, without any special software at all. The main problem with archival computing in the past has been the large amounts of data storage required, and of course the cost of this.

This problem has largely been solved by the progress of technology. As far as storage capacity is concerned, some microcomputers can now store virtually as much data as a medium sized archives service needs, by the aid of hard disks. A stand-alone microcomputer system for an archives service is no longer outside consideration, especially since the microcomputers can be networked to provide multi-site access. Equally, very capacious on-line data storage is now normally provided with mainframe computers, so that archivists can use their employers' machines without causing congestion.

In the same way, the expense of data storage is much reduced. In the case of hard disks on microcomputer, the cost is little more than the initial purchase price of the disk and its drive, which is a sum within the normal range of prices charged for office equipment. The development of on-line storage within mainframe computers has meant that the practice of writing data files on to magnetic tape for longer-term storage has now declined. It may be desirable for archivists to suggest to their computing service that an 'archiving' facility should be installed. This term is well understood in the computer world, and means the practice of moving data files which are not in immediate use, away from current storage devices and writing them on to tape. The tape is then stored in reels in a separate library, and can be brought back on-line, after a little delay, if the necessary command is given through the terminal.

The drift of this discussion is that while there is no special hardware requirement for archive work, a suitable system will have close access to its data base through a terminal (whether that be a microcomputer or a dedicated terminal). Further reflection may suggest that a desirable extension should be towards multi-site access by other terminals: this would be useful in RM, and in archives management might cause a valuable change in work habits. The preparation and input of data will remain one of the main difficulties in any computer system, so that if terminals were to be available to members of the archives team, they might find it most convenient, after some practice, to enter their own data direct to their own keyboard. One freelance archives service already does this, and maintains a portable satellite terminal which can be taken to the work site.[21]

Word (or text) processors are ideal for certain aspects of archives work, whether they stand alone or are linked to computer systems as input/output devices. Archival descriptions are ideal material for word processing: they have to be edited on input, are constantly liable to correction and updating, have to be printed out anew on the appearance of a new demand, and have to be published or at least produced for the use of readers in-house and remotely. These operations are what word processors were designed for. Archives services are strongly advised to abandon the wasteful and antique practice of using typewriters for their lists, even if they have no non-clerical use for the word processors that should take their place.

Output

Any data that is entered into a computer file and stored there can be printed out in some form of hard copy — usually on paper, but alternatively on some other medium such as microfiche. Several archives services use microfiche for their output, especially where there is a need to send the information through the post or to remote access points.[22]

In the conditions of today, a computer system ought to be able to print out material to a standard which will permit publication, or at least distribution directly to users. Ideally, output print ought to be camera-ready for duplication in numbers. This means that it should be in upper and lower case (this is standard for virtually all systems today), and printed out on a good quality dot matrix or type-wheel printer. It is often possible to use a cheaper printer for day-to-day printout in the office, and to channel the work to a more expensive machine for special output. If micro-computers are used this transfer may be done by sending disks to the printer site (but care should be taken at planning stage to see that systems are compatible). Data can be sent to remote users by telephone link, though it does not appear that any archives service does this as yet.

If the system provides search facilities, it may well be that the data base will gradually (or even suddenly) be used less to provide hard copy versions of the archive lists, and more to provide the specific responses to search enquiries. One archive service at present proposes to stock its searchroom with search responses, generated as the result of predicted enquiries.[23] The final situation will be one where users have direct access to the terminal, together with simple instruction on the command language, and hard copy finding aids will be phased out.[24]

Other applications in archival management

The data structure for archival description (Chapter 7), provides for data elements which are useful in two quite different ways, the description of the archives themselves as a means of intellectual control, and the management of the processes which the archives have to be subjected to. It is probably rather important that these two uses should be clearly distinguished, in the design of any particular control instrument. So far, in this chapter, the question of automating the archival descriptions has been the subject of discussion. It should also be possible to use computers to control the physical processes.

The PROMPT system at the PRO demonstrates a successful system for the control of movement of archival materials within a large office. Any user (staff member or public) obtains access to an archival entity by using a terminal to key in his or her identifying user number, followed by the reference code of the document asked for. The system checks that the document is available (and is not out to another reader, subject to closure, or undergoing repair), and reports the request, together with a location reference, to the repository staff. The system works well (with the proviso that computer breakdown is always possible, and a backup service must be ready), and can be used to provide statistics on document use. It is enormously faster than manual call systems, and allows users to call for many more documents per day than in the past, without an increase of manual staff. The system also reports the replacement of the item when it is finished with.[25]

The success of PROMPT reinforces the view taken in connection with archival description, that systems which undertake a clearly defined and limited function are more likely to succeed, in present conditions, than ambitious central data base schemes.

Any administrative process can be controlled in the same

way by a computer system. The RM systems provide, for instance, for checking records out to users and their return; for recording the periodical reviews and their outcome; counting the number of references there have been to documents in a particular series over time; and recording the overall statistics of the system. In archival management, systems can be designed for the control of conservation processes and repair, which would include booking documents out to the repair section, recording what was done, and the return of the document. Bringing up documents periodically for inspection could be included, as well as stock control of repair materials. In the same way, the issue and return of archive materials which have been lent for exhibition can be controlled, and a record made of when and where they were exhibited and whether they were recorded in a published catalogue. References to archival materials in published work can be recorded and the record annexed to the archival description.

A microform catalogue linked to the finding aids is feasible, though it is worth recording the experience of the PRO. It was intended in the original design of PROSPEC that it should contain a subrecord which would provide a microfilm catalogue. This was abandoned after experience, not because there was any technical difficulty with the subrecord, but because the resulting catalogue was too sparse. It gave references to the codes of documents and parts of documents which had been filmed, but in practice users needed a considerably fuller catalogue or reference apparatus to make sense of these entries. The moral is that the final output of a system should receive full planning consideration, including experiment, at an early stage, just as much as input problems.

Finally, several archives services have taken to using their computer facilities to provide a selective mailing list for their publicity material, publications and reports. Combined with a word processing facility, a mailing list system can be used to write out and send form letters (solicitation, replies to enquiries, user information).

Discussion

One of the most important factors which must be taken account of in planning the introduction of a computer system is the question of staff attitudes and the need for training. Those who have been responsible for the planning of new systems are usually very enthusiastic about them, whereas those who have had new systems thrust upon them are usually hostile. Staff indifference or even hostility are often sufficient to cause failure of the system. If a new system is under consideration, the minimum consideration for the staff would demand that they should all be consulted at an early stage, and at later critical points. The effect of the new system on the work habits of each member of staff should be considered, and allowance made for necessary adjustments.

However, an even more positive approach than this is possible. This is to involve all members of staff in the analysis required for the design of the system, and to influence the design in the direction of providing a new area of responsibility, or a new area of work, for each professional. If the new system can move the team in the direction of more collegiality, it is likely to improve its collective performance. At their best, computer systems have this ability to catalyse enthusiasm and new systems thought.

The other general comment to be made concerns backlog. Backlog accumulation is a problem endemic to all archive work: the mass of uncatalogued material which has come to the repository in a large consignment; or the mass of material which has been processed and described inadequately or to obsolete standards in the past. There are rarely sufficient resources to deal with backlog, even if there is no question of introducing new systems.

There is no satisfactory solution to this problem. In some cases it may be possible to take on extra temporary staff to deal with it. In other cases, less satisfactory expedients might include making summary descriptions in the hope that eventually full ones can be made. In any case, when a new description system is adopted (whether manual or automatic) the decision must be made whether to attempt the conversion of the old finding aids, or to cover the uncatalogued backlog, or whether to leave this area for separate treatment.

No general advice can be given on this point, except to point out that it is standard practice in the library world to begin new cataloguing systems at a specific point, and leave the old catalogue as a non-accruing file. Users must then consult two catalogues in order to be sure that they have checked everything, but (in a library context) the relative activity of the old catalogue declines with time. In the case of archives, the old catalogue probably retains its importance indefinitely, so it is a balance of inconvenience. Difficulties with backlogs exist also with manual systems.

By comparison with other information services, archives have not given much emphasis to the study of user needs.[1] This is probably due to the nature of the materials, which to a certain extent cannot be influenced by a perception of user interests. The archives are what they are: if researchers come along who are interested in them, so much the better; if not, then posterity may be assumed to have needs. In addition, many archives services were founded as an adjunct to, or in close association with, movements in academic study, which meant that the archivists and their users were in close association. All the assumptions behind these traditions can now be questioned.

In the first place, the archives of today are chosen from an increasingly huge mass of records by an increasingly stringent process of appraisal.[2] It is true that appraisal can only select from pre-existing records, and therefore cannot shape the content of an archive with complete freedom, but it can establish definitions, (or impose a bias) which ultimately must be affected by some perception of user needs. Also, many archives services may choose their sources of intake with an eye to completing their holdings in subject areas they feel to be in need of reinforcement. Local archives services set up field work projects which cover landed estates, manufacturing businesses, churches, political parties, and so on. Their aim is to provide an archive which documents the life, or widely ranging and mutually balanced aspects of life, in their region.

Specialist archives services do the same. Fieldwork projects are set up with the aim of finding accumulations of additional materials to reinforce their holdings, and strengthen the value of those holdings for research. Archives services which relate only to one organisation, such as those of research institutes or governments, may at first sight be in a more limited situation. In practice, many of these do in fact accept, or even seek for, accessions of reinforcing materials from external sources. The PRO, for example, has accepted the private (or at least semi-official) papers of public personalities, and the archives of public institutions not covered by the public records acts. They do this in order to improve the subject coverage of their holdings, and therefore, ultimately, to respond to the estimated needs of their users.

The close association between academic users and archivists which existed in the heyday of interest in early medieval administrative studies has largely faded away, but it has been replaced by a wider and looser association with academic groups. The major archives services are important agents of research, and put significant efforts into research projects. The most important of these projects involve publication of archival texts, or of lists of sources for specific subjects. Other projects, however, are aimed at developing user services. The NARS conferences of the 1970s are a good example of this kind of activity,[4] but many other kinds can be observed. In Britain the annual sequence of conferences organised by the British Records Association could be said to perform a similar function.[5] Despite the relative lack of systematic user studies, there is a great deal of user-related activity in the archive world.

Access facilities

A searchroom in which archival materials are produced for study by external readers is standard equipment for any archives service. The great expansion in the numbers of users which has occurred over the last decade means that there is now much experience in running searchroom services. These have changed and adapted under pressure, but still remain recognisably the same as they were originally designed to be. The searchrooms at the new PRO in Kew are lighter and larger than the old ones in Chancery Lane. The finding aids have been moved out into a reference room nearby, so as to reduce noise and movement. Otherwise there has been no essential change. The searchroom remains what it was: a reading room supervised by an invigilator, and with a counter where staff can control the issue and return of documents. As far as design and construction are concerned, there has been no significant alteration. Changes, however, there have been.

Firstly, there are now more searchrooms than there were. It has increasingly become accepted, for example, that records centres may need a searchroom, and should therefore offer basic access facilities for users, whether internal or external. The federal records centres in the USA led the way in this direction, and the design was taken up by large-scale records centres, where they existed, in Britain.[6]

Secondly, searchrooms have customarily been given much more technology. In the PRO the processes of document production have been automated; elsewhere materials may be produced in microform. Copying projects and the sale of microfilm copies of important sources have increased access points where microfilm readers must be used. Many records now exist only in microform, or in machine-readable media. Microfilming for purposes of conservation is now common. Photocopying facilities for users are taken for granted. The public has become accustomed to using all these machines.

Thirdly, there has been erosion of customary standards for the production of archival documents. The practice of issuing them for access by certain users at places other than the supervised searchroom has grown with the development of RM services. In RM it has always been customary to issue records to their originating departments on request. It is hard not to extend this service when the records have become archives; indeed it was always accepted in principle in manuals of archive administration.

Fourthly, archives in specialised formats are now increasingly managed by both general and specialised archives services. Film, videotape, audio materials, and photographs have all developed such services. The access facilities demanded of a photographic archive are typical of the new approach. The users of these, which include television producers, journalists, research teams supporting media projects, and other people in a hurry, have quite different expectations of the services provided by the archives, than have more traditional users. These expectations cover all aspects of the service: acquisition, arrangement, storage, access facilities, finding aids, supporting services, and expert advice.

Access restrictions

There must always be some restriction on access to archives, and even more, on access to records. This does not mean that archives and records services do not have to provide access at all stages, to certain classes of user. The traditional view, that archives become open for access after the lapse of a pre-established number of years (currently in Britain thirty years for most records), has now been considerably eroded.

Records management services must of course aim at maximising the use of their material, by authorised users, at as

183

early a stage in their lifetime as possible. These privileged users ('compiler-users' in the phrase of B. Delmas[7]) may not be confined to officials of the creating organisation, but may include members of current research enterprises. Similarly, archival material to which access is restricted because of the special confidentiality of the data, may also be the subject of specially authorised research. It would be desirable if the archives service were involved in such projects at the planning stage, and if this particular use of the archives were to be conceived from the beginning as one of the reasons for the existence of that service.

These intrusions into the traditional pattern of access control have tended to lessen the idea of archives as purely historical. Archives do, of course, give a retrospective view, but not necessarily more so than many other information media. Once a thing is recorded, it passes into history.

User rights

It has never been questioned that users have rights, which may be exercised by and through the user facilities provided by an archives service. In practice, these rights are limited not only by shortage of resources — short opening hours, for instance — but by the perceived needs of the service. If the searchroom is closed temporarily so that the archives staff can complete some cataloguing task, that is to limit the rights of one set of users with the aim of serving another set. Users' rights over the service are therefore negotiable. It may be important to try to define them.

Firstly, users (or some users) have legal rights. There are some categories of public archive to which there is a legal right of access. As S.C. Newton has pointed out, there are few of these, and the right is less well established on examination than it might have appeared.[8] Legal rights are tending to be strengthened by recent or proposed legislation on freedom of information and data protection.

Data protection already exists, but is confined to data recorded in machine-readable form. A member of the public is entitled to demand access to data bases which record information about himself, and to have that information altered if it is incorrect. The purpose of the data base must be declared when it is created, and it must be destroyed when that purpose is attained, unless there is a stated intention to use it for purposes of research. A registrar of data bases exists to protect these rights.

Freedom of information legislation has been in operation for some years in a few countries, notably Australia, Sweden and the USA. This gives the public rights of access to records of all types, and not only to machine-readable data bases, and these rights of access are not restricted to data relating to the individual mentioned in the record. Users may apply for access to specific documents, such as files held in government record systems, and this must be granted within a stated period unless a case can be made out, usually on security grounds, for withholding it. Although there have been fears that rights of this kind would interfere with the smooth running of RM systems, and might introduce bias into archives, experience so far has shown that both archivists and governments can live with these provisions.

Beyond these legal rights, actual or desirable, users have other rights based on general ethics. They have a right to expect that publicly provided archives services should provide a suitable system of finding aids, and suitable conditions in which to consult archives. These broad statements have never been defined, and existing standards are very variable. A suitable finding aid system would presumably include explanatory material to help users understand it. Users, or potential users, might also have some basis for expecting that finding aids should use established terminology and standards of layout, procedure and design. The development of networks of and between archives services of like kinds might also be seen as the legitimate expectation of users collectively.

It has been noted that archives services have often displayed a 'suicidal urge . . . to co-operate most when the co-operation benefits the researchers and least when it benefits our institutions'.[9] The examples quoted are that while archives services are generally willing to share information about holdings, they are unwilling to co-operate in acquisition policies or in the standardisation of finding aids.

User studies

Recent examination of the position of user studies in the training of information professionals has tended to emphasise the relationship between these studies and aspects of management, particularly of marketing studies.[10] This suggestion is something quite new in the context of archives

185

services, though there is a well-established tradition in librarianship.[11] The link between marketing studies, the investigatory techniques developed by the social sciences, and the study of user groups is one that certainly should be used by archivists. The users of archives, like those of library and documentation services, must belong either to unspecified and general social groupings, to organised and labelled specialist groups, or to invisible colleges which can be at least broadly defined. They are therefore suitable for study by research projects using established research techniques. At present user relations represent a serious difficulty to archivists. The great pressure for user facilities, coming at a time when resources are particularly scarce, and when the archive materials themselves need more management, is leading to a crisis. Existing services and facilities are becoming less efficient as a result.

The greatest pressure from users comes from loosely recognisable groups such as family historians or genealogists. It is curious that archivists have not been willing, on the whole, to accept these as legitimate or worthy user groups. Possibly this may be because these are interests which have developed independently of the initiative of archivists in the past. Where effort has been put into developing such subjects as academically based local studies, or demographic history, the public has taken the matter into its own hand and decided to look up its ancestors. The problems imported by pressure from these users, however, will not be solved until the archivists decide to participate in the research. There are three aspects to the problem: the organisation of the user services within the archives; the education and disciplining of the user group; and the provision of resources. These three problems are inter-related and will be solved, if at all, together.[12]

User education

User education, as an aspect of extension programmes, is a very traditional part of archival activity. Most archives services have put out some material aimed at improving the response of users.[13] The tradition has been extended into specialist areas, for example into the development of archives services for schools.[14] Experience has tended to show that these efforts are better rewarded when they are undertaken co-operatively or jointly with the user education of other

186

services. In school education, the movement which in the 1960s led to much use of archival material in teaching, has to a great extent merged into the much larger movement for the provision of all kinds of resource material for teachers. The occasional publication of archive teaching units has now become the widespread provision of teachers' resource centres, and the general adoption of revised syllabuses.[15]

User education is not confined to the outreach or extension aspects of an archives service. It should also cover users who are to a greater or less extent already inside the system: administrative users of records; professional or skilled researchers ('regular customers'); and the staff of the archives service itself, considered as users.

The first of these groups, the administrative user, is probably the most urgently in need of an education activity. Some of the techniques of information specialists may prove suitable for extension to archives or RM services. For example, an SDI exercise might well be suitable at least for specialist archives services. This technique consists in matching document and user 'profiles'.[16] The profile of a document, for this kind of purpose, would be composed of keywords derived from its archival description. A user profile could be constructed from appropriate keywords after an interview or after studying job descriptions. User profiles can also be made up from questionnaires, and this would allow the technique to be extended to users other than those who are officers of the employing organisation. The matching process should provide for flows of information in response to user requests, but also in response to unsolicited notification by the archives service. Matching profiles can be done by computer, but also manually.

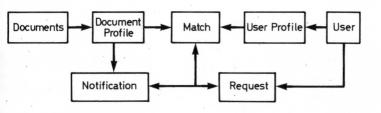

Source: B.C. Vickery, p. 197

Users who are already members of invisible colleges associated with the archives service may also be the subject of SDI operations. In addition, the archives staff may seek to develop these colleges by participation in them: indeed, this is widely done. One outcome may be to get additional resources to undertake a publications programme, or to organise seminars or conferences at which the research content of the programme can be extended. A logical development would be that the archives service would edit a periodical, either of the newsletter type, or a scientific journal. This possibility is recognised by many archives services, which issue newsletters or − less frequently − journals, but a common fault is lack of close association with relevant research groups outside the service. The more specialised the archives service, the more likely it is to be closely in touch with a user group.[17]

Staff users are the least likely to receive specific training. The proper area of investigation here is the interface between the archivist designing finding aids, and the user seeking for information through them; in other words, the match between data derived from descriptive work and the subject enquiries met with in the searchroom. It is in this area that research is particularly needed.[18]

> We have to match requests for information with patterns of retrieval designed to have application and relevance to as many cohorts of users as possible.[19]

Total archives

None of the problems discussed in this book will be solved in traditional terms. This is because the concept of the archive is in process of changing radically. Traditionally, archives were textual documents, mainly on paper, which had undergone a period of maturation. At the end of this period they were apt material for historical studies. The new concept of the archive embraces new media, does not depend on a period of maturation, and involves a process of conscious selection. The archive is then seen as something chosen by society, acting through its appointed agents.

The best progress towards the formulation of goals for the total archive has been made in Canada, where the administrative and constitutional position of the Public Archives service has stimulated integrated user-oriented activities more than elsewhere. H.A. Taylor summarises the aims of total archives in this way:

1. The acquisition of documents to reflect all aspects of social activity.
2. Acquisition of all media of record.
3. Involvement in the entire life cycle of records, through a records management programme.
4. Involvement in expanding networks for the interchange of information and strategic planning.[20]

The concept of 'media of record' would cover, in particular, photographs, film, sound media, paintings, drawings, prints, maps and machine-readable archives. This list should be extended to include books and documents which have passed an appraisal test and have been acquired by libraries of record. The whole amounts to the national archive, but the relationships between the services which maintain this archive still demand examination.

The central principle of archives administration remains that of delegation. This was discussed in the early chapters of this book. The principle requires that archival series should be managed as a continuous operation. This places archives services of the PAT type in strong contrast with libraries and archives services of the HMT type. In the context of total archives, the distinction remains important since it is the archivist's contribution to emphasise the value of provenance and original context. If the media of record are separated and administered independently by specialist institutions, there will be loss. Here is yet another argument for the close association of information services.

References

Chapter 1

1. Jenkinson, C.H., *A manual of archive administration* 1st ed., 1922; 2nd ed. revised, Lund Humphries, 1965.
2. Schellenberg, T.R., *Modern archives, principles and techniques*, University of Chicago Press, 1956.
3. Benedon, W., *Records management*, The Trident Shop, California State University, 1969.
4. Cook, M., *Archives administration*, Dawson, 1977.
5. Society of American Archivists, *Basic Manual* series, Chicago, from 1977.
6. The Grigg Report: *Report of the committee on departmental records*, HMSO, 1954 (Cmd. 9163).
7. Evans, F.B., 'Modern concepts of archives administration and records management', *Unesco Bulletin for Libraries*, 24 (1970), pp. 242—7.
8. Posner, E., *American state archives*, Chicago, 1964.
9. Roper, M., 'Modern departmental records and the record office', *JSA*, 4 (1972), pp. 400—12.
10. Evans, F.B., *Writings on archives published by and with the assistance of UNESCO: a RAMP study*, Unesco, Paris, 1983.
11. International Council on Archives, *Proceedings of the Round Table on Archives*, twice every four years from 1954.
12. Rhoads, J.B., 'New archival techniques', *Archivum*, 14 (1974), pp. 77—134.
13. Bartle, R. and Cook, M., *Computer applications in archives: a survey*, BLRDD report no. 5749, University Archives Unit, University of Liverpool, 1983.
14. National Council on Libraries, Archives and Documentation Services, *Plan for a national documentation, information and library system for Jamaica*, Kingston, Jamaica, 1978.
15. Government of Jamaica, *Records management handbook: disposition of government records*, Office of the Prime Minister, Jamaica Archives and Records Department, 1981.

16. Rhoads, J.B., *The role of archives and records management in national information systems: a RAMP study*, Unesco, Paris, 1983.
17. HMC, *Record repositories in Great Britain*, 7th ed., HMSO, 1982.
18. Foster, J. and Sheppard, J., *British archives: a guide to archive resources in the United Kingdom*, Macmillan, 1983.
19. Cook, M. and Grant, K.C., *A manual of archival description*, University of Liverpool, 1985 (in preparation).
20. Sources for definitions are summarised in Cook, M., op. cit., 1977, pp. 1–11.
21. Berner, R.C., *Archival theory and practice in the United States: a historical analysis*, University of Washington, Seattle, 1983.
22. Foskett, A.C., *The subject approach to information*, Clive Bingley, London, 4th ed., 1982, p. 6.

Chapter 2

1. d'Olier, J.H. and Delmas, B., *Planning national infrastructures for documentation, libraries and archives*, Unesco, Paris, 1975.
2. Summarised in Evans, F.B., op. cit., 1983.
3. Wright, J.R.C., 'An informative description of archives in East and West Germany', *History*, 53 (1968), pp. 385–8.
4. Pitson, C., 'The application of business management techniques to archives', Paper to X International Congress on Archives, Bonn, 1984.
5. Sewell, P., Mabbs, A.W. and Broome, E.M., *National information systems: establishing a legislative framework for the implementation of NATIS*, Unesco, Paris, 1977.
6. Published in five volumes of *Archivum*: Vol. I, Europe, Part I, Allemagne-Islande (17, 1971); Europe, Part II, Italie-Yougoslavie (19, 1972). Vol. II, Africa-Asia (20, 1972). Vol. III, America-Oceania (21, 1973). Archival legislation 1970–1980 (28, 1982).
7. Public Records Act 1958, c.51. British legislation is summarised in *Archivum* 17, pp. 173–208 and 28, pp. 387–407.
8. Cited in Cook, M., op. cit., 1977, p. 13.

9. Prasad, S.N., 'The liberalisation of access and use', *Archivum* 26 (1979), pp. 137–160.
10. Data Protection Act 1984, c.35. See also Bourn, C. and Benyon, J. (eds), *Data protection: perspectives on information privacy*, University of Leicester, Continuing Education Unit, 1983.
11. British Museum Act 1753, 26 Geo II, c.22. The current statute is the British Library Act 1972, c.54.
12. Ministère des Affaires Culturelles, Association des Archivistes français, *Manuel d'archivistique*, Paris, 1970.
13. Serjeant, W.R., 'The survey of local archive services 1968', *JSA*, 4 (1971), pp. 300–26. A later survey was carried out but not published.
14. Public Libraries and Museums Act 1964, c.75.
15. Serjeant, W.R., op. cit., Society of Archivists annual returns of salaries and staffing, c.1975–date.
16. *Methodologies in specialised archives*, Papers read at a SRG seminar, 16 April 1983, at Canterbury, SRG Occasional Papers no. 1.
17. *The newsletter of the Society of Archivists*, no. 18 (August 1981), p. 7; also subsequent issues.
18. Bott, M. and Edwards, J.A., *RM in British universities: a survey with some suggestions*, University of Reading, 1978.
19. Proceedings of a joint seminar, SRG/SAG, at Herstmonceux Castle, October 1984.
20. Proceedings of Business Archives Council conferences, 1983, 1984. BAC, 1984.
21. Jones, H.G., 'Presidential libraries: is there a case for a national presidential library?', *AA* 38 (1975), pp. 325 –8. Evans, F.B., *The National Archives and Records Service and its research resources: a select bibliography*, 1974.
22. Maike, W. and Ansell, L.J., *The small archive, a handbook for church, order and school archivists and historical societies*, Church Archivists Society, Toowoomba, Australia, 1984.
23. Foster, J. and Sheppard, J., op. cit.
24. d'Olier, J.H. and Delmas, B., op. cit. Cook, M., *Professional training needs for archivists in the Caribbean region*, Unesco, Paris, 1981, p. 5.
25. Cook, M., *Guidelines for curriculum development in records management and the administration of modern archives: a RAMP study*, Unesco, Paris, 1982.

26. General Information Programme. Meeting of experts on the harmonisation of archival training programmes, Paris, 26—30 November 1979: *Final report*, Unesco, Paris, 1980. International symposium on harmonization of education and training programmes in information science, librarianship and archival studies: *Final report*, Unesco, Paris, 1984.

27. Wasserman, P., *The teaching of management as a subject for the preparation of librarians, documentalists, archivists and other information specialists*. Cook, M., *The teaching of technology . . .*; and Sene, H., *The teaching of user studies . . .*, Papers at the above-mentioned symposium, Unesco, 1984.

28. British Standards Institution, *Conservation of documents*, BS 4971, 1973; *Recommendations for the storage and exhibition of documents*, BS 5454, 1977.

29. Duchein, M., *Archive buildings and equipment*, K.G. Saur, Munich, 1977.

Chapter 3

1. The principal study of RM in a government context is Schellenberg, T.R., *Modern archives, principles and techniques*, Chicago, 1956. In a business context it is Benedon, W., *Records management*, California, 1969. No recent synthesis is available, but see *Records management 1—9*, published by the Records Management Group, Society of Archivists, 1977—date; also Cook, M., *Archives administration*, Dawson, 1977, pp. 25—94, and Couture, C. and Rousseau, J.Y., *Les archives au XXe siècle*, University of Montreal, 1982.

2. Society of Archivists, RMG, *Office automation and records management*, 1981.

3. Newton, S.C., 'Selection and disposal: legal requirements', *Records Management 1*, Society of Archivists, RMG, 1977.

4. Smith, J.G., 'Archives and the food and drug industries: a preliminary notice of proposed US legislation', *Business Archives* 44 (1978), pp. 31—43.

5. Miller, D., *Health and safety in the conservation workshop*, an information leaflet to be issued by the Society of Archivists, may start a compilation of relevant statutes.

6. Cook, M., op. cit., 1977, p. 27.
7. Cook, M., *Guidelines for curriculum development* . . ., Chapters 6—7.
8. Cook, M., op. cit., 1977, p. 30. Benedon, W., op. cit., Chapter 2.
9. Cheshire Record Office, modern records management programme, 1977.
10. British Steel Corporation, transfer list; *see also* Cook, M., 1977, p. 51.
11. Tyne & Wear County Archives Service; *see also* Cook, M., *Archives and the Computer*, Butterworth, 1980, p. 60.
12. Cook, M., 'Surveying current records', *JSA*, 4(1972), pp. 413—22.
13. The Grigg Report, *Report of the committee on departmental records*, HMSO, 1954 (Cmd. 9163). The Wilson Report: *Modern public records, selection and access*, HMSO, 1981 (Cmd. 8204).
14. A commentary on the Grigg recommendations is in Cook, M., 1977, pp. 63—6.
15. Mabbs, A.W. and Duboscq, G., *The organization of intermediate records storage*, Unesco, Paris, 1974. Standards are in Gondos, V. (ed), *Reader for archives and records center buildings*, Society of American Archivists, 1970.
16. Hampson, J., 'Running a record centre', *Records management 2*, Society of Archivists, RMG, 1978, pp. 40 —59.
17. Cook, 1977, pp. 51—2.
18. Public Record Office, Records Administration Division, *Manual of records administration*, PRO, 1983.
19. *Black book of the Admiralty*, ed. Twiss, T., HMSO, 1871—76.
20. Gondos, V., op. cit., pp. 84—7.
21. Cook, 1980, pp. 55—75.
22. Bartle & Cook, op. cit., p. 4.

Chapter 4

1. Cook, M., *Guidelines*, 1982.
2. During the 1970s an agreement was reached between the Library Association, the Museums Association and the Society of Archivists, but was never put into effect in any formal way.

3. Grigg Report: see discussion in Cook, 1977, pp. 63 ff.
4. PRO, *Manual of records administration*, 1982, part 2.
5. McCoy, D.R., *The National Archives: America's ministry of documents, 1934—1968*, University of North Carolina, 1978.
6. Wilson Report, 1981. See also *Modern Public Records*, Cmd 8531, HMSO, 1982.
7. Jenkinson, H., *Manual of archive administration*, 1965, pp. 149—50.
8. Schellenberg, T.R., *Modern archives*, 1956. Discussion in Cook, 1977, pp. 67 ff.
9. Rieger, M., 'Modern records retirement and appraisal practice', *UJISLAA* 1 (1979), pp. 200—9.
10. RMG, *The records of social service departments: their retention and management*, Society of Archivists, 1982.
11. Grigg Report, sects. 105, 108.
12. Jagerskold, O., *Riksarkivet 1618—1968*, Stockholm, 1969.
13. Hull, F., *The use of sampling techniques in the retention of records: a RAMP study with guidelines*, Unesco, Paris, 1981.
14. Fishbein, M., *The National Archives and statistical research*, Ohio University Press, 1973.
15. Moss, M.S. and Hume, J.R., *The workshop of the British Empire: engineering and shipbuilding in the west of Scotland*, Heinemann, 1977.
16. Chaloner, W.H. and Richardson, R.C., *British economic and social history: a bibliographic guide*, Manchester UP, 1976.
17. Brichford, M.J., *Archives and manuscripts: appraisal and accessioning*, SAA Basic Manual series, Chicago, 1977.
18. Rapport, L., 'No grandfather clause: reappraising accessioned records', *AA* 44 (1981), pp. 143—50.
19. Brichford, M.J., op. cit., p. 2.
20. Cook, 1977, pp. 73—5.
21. Ibid, pp. 100—3.

Chapter 5

1. Jenkinson, op. cit., pp. 83 ff. Cook, 1977, pp. 103—8.
2. Schellenberg, T.R., *The management of archives*, Columbia University, 1965, p. 81; cited by Gracey,

D.B., II, *Archives and manuscripts: arrangement and description*, SAA Basic Manual series, Chicago, 1977, p. 4.

3. Schellenberg, op. cit., p. 118; cited by Cook, 1977, p. 105.
4. This section is based closely on MAD Part II. However, because of its original terms of reference, MAD treats questions of level as being in the field of description, and not that of arrangement.
5. Jenkinson, p. 101.
6. Taylor, H.A., *The arrangement and description of archives*, ICA handbooks, vol. 2, K.G. Saur, Munich, 1980.
7. Holmes, O.W., 'Archival arrangement: five different operations at five different levels', *AA* 27 (1964), pp. 21—41.
8. Scott, P.J., 'The record group concept: a case for abandonment', *AA* 29 (1966), pp. 493—504.
9. Cook, 1980, pp. 85—91.
10. Lytle, R.H., 'Intellectual access to archives: provenance and content indexing methods of subject retrieval', *AA* 43 (1980), pp. 64—75; 43 (1981), pp. 191—207. Berner, R.C., op. cit., p. 29.
11. Library of Congress, *National union catalog of manuscript collections*, Washington DC, 1959—73.
12. Bell, L., 'The new PRO at Kew', *JSA* 5 (1974), pp. 1—7.
13. Jenkinson, p. 101.
14. Scott, P.J., p. 498.
15. Godber, J., 'The county record office at Bedford', *Archives* 1 (Lady Day 1949), pp. 10—20. Emmison, F.G., 'The Essex record office', *Archives* 1 (Michaelmas 1949), pp. 8—16; Emmison, F.G. (ed), *Guide to the Essex Record Office*, Chelmsford, 1969.
16. Hull, F. (ed), *Guide to the Kent County Archives Office. First Supplement, 1957—1968*, Maidstone, 1971.
17. Based on schemes used in several local record offices, including West Sussex, Gwent, Lancashire, Hertfordshire, Durham, Leicestershire Record Offices.
18. Based on scheme used in Cheshire Record Office.
19. L. McDonald, unpublished paper for the Society of Archivists.

20. West Sussex Record Office, classification of political records.
21. Warwick University, Modern Records Centre, *Notes for researchers*.
22. Maclean, I., 'An analysis of Jenkinson's manual in the light of Australian experience', in Hollaender, A.E.J. (ed), *Essays in memory of Sir H. Jenkinson*, Society of Archivists, London, 1962, p. 144.

Chapter 6

1. This chapter is closely based on MAD, parts I & II.
2. The discussion of finding aid systems owes much to Berner, R.C., 1983.
3. Newton, S.C. (ed), *The Londonderry papers: catalogue of the documents deposited in the Durham Record Office by the 9th Marquess of Londonderry*, Durham County Council, 1969.
4. PRO, *Records of interest to social scientists 1919–1939*, PRO Handbooks 14, 1971.
5. Oxfordshire County Council, *A handlist of enclosure acts and awards relating to the county of Oxford*, Oxford, 1963.
6. Hampshire Archivists Group, *Poor law in Hampshire through the centuries: a guide to the records*, Hampshire County Council, 1970.
7. MAD, para. 10.7.
8. Walne, P., 'The record commissions, 1800–37', in Ranger, F. (ed), *Prisca munimenta: studies in archival and administrative history*, University of London Press, 1973, pp. 9–18.
9. *Government publications: British national archives*, Sectional list 24, HMSO, annually.
10. HMSO Sectional list 17.
11. *Constitutional relations between Britain and India: the transfer of power 1942–1947*, Vols. 1–12, HMSO, 1970–83.
12. Taylor, H.A., *Archival services and the concept of the user: a RAMP study*, Unesco, Paris, 1984.
13. Pugh, R.B. (ed), *The records of the colonial and dominions offices*, PRO handbooks, Vol. 3, HMSO, 1964.
14. Taylor, H.A., 1984, p. 38.

15. Roper, M., 'Modern departmental records and the record office', *JSA*, 4 (1972), pp. 400–12.
16. Methods of Listing working party, at the meeting held at the PRO, May 1984.
17. Ranger, F., 'The common pursuit', *Archives* 9 (1970), pp. 121–9.
18. Cook, C. (ed), *Sources in British political history, 1900 –1951*, Vols. 1–5, Macmillan, 1975–78.
19. Contemporary Scientific Archives Centre, progress reports 1–22.
20. HMC, *Guide to the location of collections described in the Reports and Calendars series*, HMSO, 1982. *The manuscript papers of British scientists 1600–1940*, HMSO, 1982.
21. *The national inventory of documentary sources in the UK*, Chadwyck-Healey, 1984+.
22. Roper, M., 'PROSPEC-SA: a case study in setting up a co-operative computer project', *ADPA* 2 (1977), pp. 9–14.
23. *AACR2*, Part I, Chapters 3–11.
24. *Manuscripts, a MARC format*, Library of Congress, 1973. IFLA, *ISBD (NBM): international standard bibliographic description for non-book materials*, London, 1977.
25. Austin, D., *PRECIS: a manual of concept analysis and subject indexing*, BNB, 1974.
26. IFLA, ISBD (NBM), Simmons, P. and Hopkinson, A. (eds), *CCF: the common communications format*, Unesco, 1984.
27. Hensen, S.L., *Archives, personal papers, and manuscripts: a cataloging manual for archival repositories, historical societies and manuscript libraries*, Library of Congress, 1983.
28. Khattack, M.M., *Archival control manual*, Research Libraries Group, 1984.
29. British Library, Department of Manuscripts, *Report of the working party on cataloguing*, March 1983.
30. MAD, Part III.
31. The PRO user study of 1970–1 concentrated on the impending effects of the new building at Kew. Lord Chancellor's Office, *13th annual report of the . . . PRO*, HMSO, 1972. Annual statistical analyses are carried out, e.g. *25th annual report of PRO*, HMSO, 1984.

32. Lytle, R.H., art. cit., p. 199.

Chapter 7

1. The current version of the data elements is Part III of MAD, but the MLWP continues to develop the original data standard as a basis for computerisation.
2. Khattuck, M.M., op. cit.; Hensen, S.L., op. cit.
3. *AACR2*, Part I, Chapter 1.
4. Grigg Report, pp. 12—15.
5. Jenkinson, H., op. cit., pp. 37—8.
6. This view is promoted by Mr V. Gray, Essex Record Office.
7. Hensen, S.L., op. cit., p. 14.
8. *Social history and industrial classification (SHIC), a subject classification for museum collections*, Centre for English Cultural Tradition and Language, University of Sheffield, 1983.

Chapter 8

1. Bell, L., 'Controlled vocabulary subject indexing of archives', *JSA*, 4 (1971), pp. 285—99.
2. Berner, R.C., op. cit., p. 33.
3. Bell, L., art. cit., p. 285.
4. Cox, N.S.M. and Davies, R.S., *The indexing of records in the PRO*, Newcastle upon Tyne, 1970; Hunnisett, R., *Indexing for editors*, British Records Association, London, 1972.
5. Bell, L., art. cit., p. 296.
6. Hudson, J.P., *Manuscripts indexing*, British Library Department of Manuscripts, 1979.
7. HMC, *Subject indexing schema and wordlist*, 1969.
8. Bell, L., art. cit., p. 286.
9. Cited in Edwards, T., 'Indexing LISA . . . ' in Harrod, L.M., *Indexers on indexing*, R.R. Bowker, New York, 1978, pp. 304—16.
10. Classification Research Group scheme.
11. SHIC, op. cit.
12. Information from Mrs A. Prochaska, PRO.
13. Bell, L., art. cit., p. 287.

14. Rhoads, J.B., *The applicability of UNISIST Guidelines and ISO international standards to archives administration and records management: a RAMP study*, Unesco, 1982.
15. Hunnisett, R., op. cit.; Hudson, J.P., op. cit.; *AACR2*, Part II, Chapter 22.
16. British Library, Department of Manuscripts, *Guide to the catalogues and indexes of the Department of Manuscripts*, Nickson, M.A.E. (ed), British Library, 1982.
17. Cook, M., *Archives and the computer*, 1980, p. 103.
18. Hibbins, R.V., *Cataloguing in the Department of Manuscripts, a feasibility study and proposal for the introduction of automation*, Processed paper, British Library, June 1981.
19. Bakewell, K.G.B., 'The PRECIS indexing system' in Harrod, L.M., op. cit., p. 293.
20. Bartle, R. and Cook, M., op. cit., p. 11.
21. Bell, L., 'Document requisitioning in the PRO, Kew', *JSA*, 5 (1976), p. 327.
22. Hibbins, R.V., op. cit., section 6.
23. Bearman, D., 'Automated access to archival information: assessing systems', *AA* 42 (1979), pp. 179–190.

Chapter 9

1. Cook, M., 'Applying automated techniques to archives administration', *Journal of Documentation* 39 (1983), pp. 73–84.
2. Bell, L. and Roper, M. (eds), *Proceedings of an international seminar on ADP in archives*, PRO, HMSO, London, 1975.
3. Bell, L., 'PRO survey of computer applications', *ADPA* 1 (1974), pp. 11–14.
4. Cook, M., *Archives and the computer*, 1980.
5. Bartle, R. and Cook, M., op. cit., 1983.
6. Khattack, M.M., op. cit.
7. Hibbins, R.V., op. cit.
8. PRO, *PROSPEC Manual*, McCall, F. (ed), London, nd.
9. Bartle, R. and Cook, M., op. cit., p. 18.
10. PROSPEC Manual, section 4.
11. Bartle, R. and Cook, M., p. 22.
12. Ibid, p. 48.

13. Underwood, M., 'A computer index for the archives of St John's College, Cambridge: a progress report', *JSA*, 6 (1979), pp. 214–18.
14. Bartle, R. and Cook, M., p. 28.
15. MAD, Part II.
16. Bartle, R. and Cook, M., pp. 41–4.
17. Philips, C.M. and Woolgar, C.M., *Computerising archives: some guidelines*, Society of Archivists, 1984.
18. Cook, M., 1980, pp. 93–7.
19. Glasgow University Archives, *PARCH prospectus*, 1983.
20. Porter, M.F., *GOS reference manual*, MDA, Duxford, 1981.
21. Bartle, R. and Cook, M., pp. 45–6.
22. Ibid, p. 12.
23. Ibid, p. 52.
24. Bearman, D., *AA* 42, 1979, pp. 350–1.
25. McCrank, L.J. (ed), *Automating the archives*, ASIS, White Plains, NY, 1981.

Chapter 10

1. McCrank, L.J., op. cit. p. 229.
2. *Constitution et reconstitution des patrimoines archivistiques nationaux*, Actes de la 19me Conference internationale de la Table Ronde des Archives, Cagliari, 1977, ICA, 1980.
3. Galbraith, V.H., *Studies in the public records*, Nelson, London, 1948.
4. Fishbein, M.H. (ed), *The National Archives and statistical research*, Ohio University Press, 1973.
5. Proceedings of the BRA conferences are in *Archives*, 1948 ff.
6. Gondos, V., op. cit. British Steel Corporation's brochure on records centre services at Irthlingborough (1973).
7. Delmas, B., 'User needs and archive facilities: a tentative typology and analysis', Processed paper, available from UNESCO, March 1977.
8. Newton, S.C., 'Selection and disposal: legal requirements', *Records Management 1*, Society of Archivists, RMG, 1977, pp. 43–51.
9. Citation by Taylor, H.A., *Archival services and the concept of the user: a RAMP study*, Unesco, 1984, p. 74;

of Bearman, D., *Towards national information systems: opportunities and requirements*, SAA, Chicago, 1982.

10. Sene, H., *The teaching of user studies as a subject for the preparation of librarians, documentalists, archivists and other information specialists*, International symposium on harmonization of education and training programmes in information science, librarianship and archival studies, Unesco, October-1984.

11. Ford, G., *User studies: an introductory guide and select bibliography*, University of Sheffield, Centre for Research in User Studies, 1977.

12. Genealogical service at the Public Record Office of Northern Ireland.

13. Iredale, D., *Enjoying archives*, David & Charles, Newton Abbot, 1973.

14. *A statement by the Society of Archivists on the educational use of archives*, Society of Archivists, Education Services Committee, 1980.

15. Schools Council, *History, geography and social science 8–13*, 'Place, time and society 8–13', Schools Council, 1976.

16. Vickery, B.C., *Techniques of information retrieval*, Butterworths, 1970, pp. 197–200.

17. *ESRC Data Archive bulletin*, University of Essex.

18. Lytle, R.H., *Subject retrieval in archives: a comparison of the provenance and content indexing methods*, Ph.D., Maryland, 1979.

    This is possibly the only high level specialised research into archival methodology anywhere.

19. Taylor, H.A., op. cit., 1983, p. 21.

20. Cook, T., 'The tyranny of the medium: a comment on "total archives"', *Archivaria* 9 (1980), pp. 141–50. Also Birrell, A., 'The tyranny of tradition', *Archivaria* 10 (1980), pp. 249–52. Both cited by Taylor, H.A., 1983, p. 48.

Bibliography

Archives administration: general

Bain, G., 'State archival law: a content analysis', *AA*, 46, pp. 158–174, 1983.

Berner, R.C., 'Manuscript collections and archives: a unitary approach', *Library Resources and Technical Services*, 9, pp. 213–220.

Berner, R.C., 'Manuscript collections, archives and special collections: their relationships', *Library and Archival Security*, 5, pp. 9–17, 1983.

Berner, R.C., *Archival theory and practice in the United States: a historical analysis*, University of Washington, Seattle, 1983.

Birdsall, W.F., 'Archivists, librarians and issues during the pioneering era of the American archival movement', *Journal of Library History*, 14, pp. 457–479, 1979.

Bordin, R.B. and Warner, R.M., *The modern manuscript library*, New York, 1966.

Brubaker, R.L., 'Manuscript collections' in Kujoth, J.S., *Readings in non-book librarianship*, pp. 303 ff, Scarecrow Press, Metuchen, 1968.

Burke, F.G., 'Archival co-operation', *AA*, 46, pp. 293–305, 1983.

Cook, M., *Archives administration*, Dawson, 1977.

Cook, M., *Archives and the computer*, Butterworths, 1980.

Cook, M., *Guidelines for curriculum development in records management and the administration of modern archives: a RAMP study*, UNESCO, 1982.

Cook, M. and Grant, K.C., *A manual of archival description*, University of Liverpool, 1985 (in preparation).

Couture, C. and Rousseau, J.Y., *Les archives au XXe. siècle*, University of Montreal, 1982.

Duchein, M. (comp.), *Basic international bibliography of archives administration*, ICA, K.G. Saur, 1978.

Evans, F.B. (comp.), *The administration of modern archives: a select bibliographic guide*, NARB, Washington DC, 1970.

Evans, F.B. (comp.), *The history of archives administration: a select bibliography*, UNESCO, 1979.

Evans, F.B. (ed), *Writings on archives published by or with the assistance of UNESCO: a RAMP study*, UNESCO, 1983.

Filiou, M., 'Les archives et la mise en valeur du patrimoine', *Archives*, 12, pp. 1–10, 1981.

Foster, J. and Sheppard, J., *British archives: a guide to archival resources in the UK*, Macmillan, 1982.

Hepworth, P., *Archives and manuscripts in libraries*, 2nd ed., Library Association, 1964.

Hesselager, L., 'Fringe or grey literature in the National Library: on 'papyrolatry' and the growing similarity between the materials in libraries and archives', *AA*, 47, pp. 255–270, 1984.

Hildesheimer, F., *Guidelines for the preparation of general guides to national archives: a RAMP study*, 1983.

Hobbs, J.L., *Local history and the library*, 2nd ed., Andre Deutsch/Grafton, 1973.

Hull, F., 'Foundations', *JSA*, 7, pp. 149–155, 1983.

Hull, F., 'Jenkinson and the "acquisitive record office"', *JSA*, 6, pp. 1–9, 1978.

International Council on Archives, *Dictionary of archival terminology*, ed. F.B. Evans, F.J. Himly and P. Walne, ICA Handbooks 3, K.G. Saur, 1984.

Jenkinson, C.H., *Manual of archive administration*, 2nd ed., Lund Humphries, 1965.

Knightbridge, A.A., 'National archives policy', *JSA*, 7, pp. 213–223, 1983.

McCoy, D.R., *The national archives: America's ministry of documents, 1934–1968*, University of North Carolina, Chapel Hill, 1978.

Rastic, M., *The management of smaller (local) archival institutions*, Paper to X International Congress on Archives, Bonn, 1984.

Rhoads, J.B., *The role of archives and records management in national information systems: a RAMP study*, UNESCO, 1983.

Schellenberg, T.R., *The management of archives*, New York, 1965.

Schellenberg, T.R., *Modern archives: principles and techniques*, Chicago, 1956.

Sowoolu, S.O., 'Worldwide archival expansion and evolution', *Archivum*, 26, pp. 163–170, 1979.

Storey, R., 'Establishing the archivist's identity within an organisation, Society of Archivists', SRG *Proceedings of a forum at Imperial College*, pp. 5–8, January 1983.

Vaganor, F.M. *The increasing social role of state archives in the contemporary world*, Paper to X International Congress on Archives, Bonn, 1984.

Watson, R., 'The archivist in the library — the manuscript collection', Society of Archivists, SRG *Proceedings of a forum at Imperial College*, pp. 1—4, January 1983.

Weldon, E., 'Archives and the challenge of change', *AA*, 46, pp. 125—134, 1983.

White, B. (ed), *Archives journals: a study of their coverage by primary and secondary sources*, RAMP studies and guidelines, UNESCO, 1981.

Archives administration: practice

Alegbeleye, G., 'Bibliographical control of archival and manuscript materials in Nigeria', *International Library Review*, 11, pp. 159—161, 1979.

Arad, A. and Bell, L., 'Archival description: a general system', *ADPA*, 2, pp. 2—9, 1978.

Batty, C.D., 'Perspectives from information science' in McCrank, L.J. (ed), *Automating the Archives*, p. 271.

Baudot, M., *Les instruments de recherche*, in Ministère des affaires culturelles, *Manuel d'archivistique*, Paris, pp. 243—293, 1970.

Bell, L., 'Archival accommodation in UK', *JSA*, 6, pp. 345—364, 1980.

Bell, L., 'Controlled vocabulary subject indexing of archives', *JSA*, 4, pp. 285—299, 1971.

Berner, R.C. and Haller, U., 'Principles of archival inventory construction', *AA*, 47, pp. 134—155, 1984.

Berner, R.C., 'The record group concept', *Georgia Archives*, Winter 1976.

Biljan, F., *Finding aids in service of research*, Report of VII International Congress of Archives, Moscow, 1972.

Boles, F., 'Disrespecting original order', *AA*, 45, pp. 26—32, 1982.

Booth, P.F. and South, M.L., *Information filing and finding*, Elm Publications, Buckden (Cambs), 1982.

British Library working party on classification and indexing, Final report, BLR & DD report no. 5233, 1976.

British Library, Department of Manuscripts, *Report of working party on cataloguing*, Processed paper, 1983.

Bryant, P., 'The library catalogue: key or combination lock?', *Catalogue and Index*, 67, pp. 1–7, 1982.

Chalmers, C.D. and Post, J.B., 'A flexible system for the cumulative general index', *JSA*, 6, pp. 482–492, 1981.

Chalmers, D., 'Computer indexing in the Public Record Office', *JSA*, 6, pp. 399–413, 1980.

CITRA, 'Normes a respecter pour l'establissement et l'organisation des institutions d'archives', *Actes des 19e. conference internationale de la table ronde des archives*, Gosier, 1979, 1981.

Coveney, D.K., 'The cataloguing of literary manuscripts', *Journal of Documentation*, 6 (1950).

Cox, R.J., 'Bibliography and reference for the archivist', *AA*, 46, pp. 185–187, 1983.

D'Huart, S., 'Les archives privées: essai de méthodologie', *Gazette des Archives*, 110, pp. 167–176, 1980.

Davies, R., 'Documents, information, or knowledge? Choices for librarians', *Journal of Librarianship*, 15, pp. 47–65, 1983.

Dinel, G., 'L'archiviste: un professionel de l'information', *Argus*, 9, pp. 143–146, 1980.

Evans, F.B. and Ketelaar, E. (eds.), *A guide for surveying archival and records management systems and services: a RAMP study*, UNESCO, 1983.

Frost, C.O., *Cataloguing nonbook materials: problems in theory and practice*, ed. by A.T. Dowell, Libraries Unlimited, Littleton (Colo), 1983.

Gorman, M. and Winkler, P.W. (eds.), *Anglo-American Cataloguing Rules*, 2nd ed., Library Association, 1978.

Gracy, D.B., II, *Archives and manuscripts: arrangement and description*, SAA Basic Manuals, 1977.

Harrod, L.M. (ed), *Indexers on indexing*, Society of Indexers, R.R. Bowker, 1978.

Hensen, S.L., *Archives, personal papers and manuscripts: a cataloguing manual for archival repositories, historical societies and manuscript libraries*, Library of Congress, Washington DC, 1983.

Hoffman, H.H., 'AACR2 and the level of description principle', *Library Resources and Technical Services*, 27, pp. 395–396, 1983.

Holbert, S.E. *Archives and manuscripts: reference and access*, SAA Basic Manuals, 1977.

Holmes, O.W., 'Archival arrangement: five different operations at five different levels', *AA*, 27, pp. 21–41 (1964).

IFLA, *Working group on international and standard biblio-graphic description for nonbook materials*, ISBD(NBM), IFLA, International office for UBC, 1977.

Kepley, D.R., 'Sampling in archives: a review', *AA*, 47, pp. 237–242, 1984.

Khattack, M.M., *Archival control manual*, Research Libraries Group, 1984.

Light, R., 'Use of the draft archival data standard to design record media', *ADPA*, 4, pp. 105–108, 1982–3.

Lovett, R.W., 'Care and handling of non-governmental arch-ives', *Library Trends*, 5 (1957).

Lucas, L., 'Efficient finding aids: developing a system for control of archives and manuscripts', *AA*, 44, pp. 21–26, 1981.

Lytle, R.H., *Subject retrieval in archives: a comparison of the provenance and content indexing methods*, PhD, Univer-sity of Maryland, 1979.

Maher, W.J., 'Measurement and analysis of processing costs in academic archives', *College & Research Libraries*, 43 (1982), pp. 59–67 (1982).

Maike, W. and Ansell, L.J., *The small archive: a handbook for church, order and school archivists and historical societies*, Church Archivists Society, Toowoomba, 1984.

Marco, G.A., 'Bibliographic control of library and inform-ation science literature', *Libri*, 33, pp. 45–60, 1983.

Naud, G. and Naud, C., 'L'analyse des archives contempor-aines', *Gazette des Archives*, 115, pp. 216–245, 1981.

Nedobity, W., 'Terminology and its application to classifica-tion, indexing and abstracting', *UJISLAA* 5, pp. 227–234, 1983.

Orna, E., 'Information management in museums: there's more to it than documentation and computers', *Museums Journal*, 82, pp. 79–82, 1982.

Orna, E., *Build yourself a thesaurus*, Running Angel, Nor-wich, 1983.

Papritz, J., *Current methods of archive classification, pre-1800 material*, Report to V International Congress on Archives, Brussels, 1964.

Pitson, C., *The application of business management techni-ques to archives*, Paper to X International Congress on Archives, Bonn, 1984.

Powers, T.E., 'Processing as reconstruction: the Philip A. Hart senatorial collection' *AA*, 46 (1983), pp. 183–185.

Rhoads, J.B., 'Standardization for archives', *UJISLAA*, 3, pp. 165–169, 1981.

Roper, M., 'The PRO and its means of reference', *Indexer*, 12, pp. 146—147, 1981.

Roper, M., *Expert consultation on the development of a long-term plan for the preparation of archival and records management guidelines, standards and norms: report*, Bari, Italy, PRO, unpublished paper, September 1979.

SAA, *Archival forms manual*, Chicago, 1982.

SAA, *Inventories and registers: a handbook of techniques and examples: a report of the committee on finding aids*, SAA, Chicago, 1976.

SAA, NSTIFS, *Data elements used in archives, manuscripts, and records repository information systems: a dictionary of standard terminology*, SAA, 1982.

Scott, P.J., Smith, C.D. and Finlay, G., 'Archives and administrative change: some methods and approaches', *Archives and Manuscripts*, 8, pp. 51—69, 1980.

Seal, A., *Automated cataloguing in the UK*, BLR & DD Report no. 5545, University of Bath, 1980.

Seal, A., Bryant, P. and Hall, C., *Full and short entry catalogues: library needs and uses*, Bath University, Centre for Catalogue Research, 1982.

Smith, D., *Systems thinking in library and information management*, K.G. Saur/Clive Bingley, 1980.

Society of Archivists, *The preparation of finding aids. Correspondence course papers*, n.d.

Southampton University Library, *The Wellington papers: guide to the data base*, Processed paper, 1984.

Specialist Repositories Group, *Methodologies in specialised archives*, Society of Archivists, SRG occasional papers, no. 1, 1983.

Storey, R., 'Indexing archives', *The Indexer*, 5, pp. 159—168, 1967.

Swift, M., *Management and technical resources*, Paper to X International Congress on Archives, Bonn, 1984.

Szedo, A., 'Modern systems of classification for contemporary archives later than 1800', *Archivum*, 14, pp. 57—68, 1964.

Taylor, H.A., *The arrangement and description of archival materials*, K.G. Saur, 1980.

Turnbaugh, R.C., 'Living with a guide', *AA*, 46, pp. 449—452 (1983).

Vickery, B.C., *Techniques of information retrieval*, Butterworth, 1970.

Wimalaratne, K.D.G., *Scientific and technological information in transactional files in government records and archives: a RAMP study*, UNESCO, 1984.

Automation and technology

'RLIN developments in archives and manuscript records', *Outlook on Research Libraries*, 6, pp. 14–15 (1984).

Arad, A. and Olsen, M.E., *An introduction to archival automation*, ICA, Automation Committee, 1981.

Ashton, D., *Machine-readable records for permanent preservation: in Sampling PIP's, proceedings of a seminar, Jan. 1984*, PRO, RAD Occasional paper no. 8, 1984.

Attig, J.C., 'The concept of a MARC format', *Information Technology and Libraries*, 2, pp. 7–17, 1983.

Bartle, R. and Cook, M., *Computer applications in archives: a survey*, Liverpool University, 1983.

Bearman, D., 'Functional specifications of an integrated information managment system for administering a program for active archival or manuscript records', *Part I, Overview of systems activity: a report to the SAA National Information Systems Task Force*, Smithsonian Institution, August 1982.

Bell, L., 'Archival implications of machine-readable records', *Archivum*, 26, pp. 85–92, 1979.

Blair, J. and Riden, P., 'Computer-assisted analysis of medieval deeds', *Archives*, 15 (1982), pp. 195–208.

Bradler, R., 'Computerised access to both archival and library materials', *INSPEL*, 16, pp. 97–102, 1982.

Dodd, S.A., *Cataloguing machine-readable data files: an interpretative manual*, ALA, Chicago, 1982.

Dolgih, F.I. and Mihailov, O.A., 'Computers in the state archives of the USSR', *UJISLAA*, 5, pp. 235–242, 1983.

Duerr, W.T., 'Some thoughts and designs about archives and automation, 1984', *AA*, 47, pp. 271–290, 1984.

Fishbein, M.H., *Guidelines for administering machine-readable archives*, ICA, Automation Committee, 1980.

Geda, C.L., Austin, E.W. and Blouin, F.X., *Archivists and machine-readable records*, SAA, 1980.

Griffiths, J.M., Main trends in information technology, *UJISLAA*, 4, pp. 230–238, 1982.

Hendley, A.M., *The archival storage potential of microfilm, magnetic media and optical data discs: a comparison based on a literature review*, NRCd, Hertford, 1983.

Hendriks, K.B., *The presentation and restoration of photographic materials in archives and libraries: a RAMP study with guidelines*, UNESCO, 1984.

Hickerson, H.T., *Archives and manuscripts: an introduction to automated access*, SAA Basic Manuals, 1981.

Hockey, S., *A guide to computer applications in the humanities*, Duckworth, 1980.

ICA Automation Committee, *Elementary terms in archival automation*, Koblenz, 1983.

Keene, J.A. and Roper, M., *Planning, equipping and staffing a document reprographic service: a RAMP study with guidelines*, UNESCO, 1984.

Keene, J.A., 'Microform and computer-based systems in current use in the PRO', *International Journal of Micrographics and Video Technology*, 1, pp. 179—182, 1982.

Kenney, A.R., 'Archival co-operation: a critical look at statewide archival networks', *AA*, 46, pp. 414—432 (1983).

Kesner, R.M. and Jones, C.H., *Microcomputers applications in libraries: a management tool for the 1980s and beyond*, Greenwood Press, Westport, Conn., 1984.

Kesner, R.M., 'Automated information management: is there a role for the archivist in the office of the future?', *ADPA*, 4, pp. 59—70 (1984).

Kesner, R.M., 'Microcomputer applications in archives: towards an international retrieval system', *ADPA*, 4, pp. 57—66 (1982—3).

Kesner, R.M., 'Microcomputer archives and records management systems: guidelines for future development', *ADPA*, 3, pp. 41—54 (1981).

Kesner, R.M., *Automation for archivists and records managers: planning and implementation strategies*, ALA, Chicago, 1984.

Kesner, R.M., *Automation, machine-readable records and archival administration: an annotated bibliography*, SAA, 1980.

Khattack, M.M., *Archival control manual*, Research Libraries Group, February 1984.

Kula, S., *The archival appraisal of moving images: a RAMP study with guidelines*, UNESCO, 1983.

Lambert, M., 'L'informatique aux archives nationales, Association des bibliotécaires français', *Bulletin d'Informations*, 110, p. 25, 1981.

Library of Congress, MARC development office, *Manuscripts: a MARC format: specifications for magnetic tapes containing catalog records for single manuscripts or manuscript collections*, by L.S. Maruyama, Washington DC, 1973.

Long, A., 'UK/MARC and US/MARC: a brief history and comparison', *Journal of Documentation*, 40, pp. 1–12, 1984.

McCrank, L.J. (ed), *Automating the archives: issues and problems in computer applications*, Knowledge Industry Publications, 1981.

Middleton, M., 'Archives and computers: description and retrieval', *Archives and Manuscripts*, 9, pp. 53–65 (1981).

Mitchell, S.P. and Manojilovich, S., 'Machine-readable archives user surveys', *ADPA*, 4, pp. 67–76, 1982–3.

O'Neill, J.E., *Automation of archival finding aids*, Paper to X International Congress on Archives, Bonn, 1984.

Philips, C.M. and Woolgar, C.M., *Computerising archives: some guidelines*, Society of Archivists, 1984.

Pitson, C., *ADP in the Australian Archives: managing information about government records*, Paper to X International Congress on Archives, Bonn, 1984.

Prowse, S., *Software for producing library keyword catalogues: a description of selected packages*, Elsevier International Bulletins, Oxford, 1983.

Public Record Office, *The selection and preparation for transfer of machine-readable records: a provisional guide*, PRO, n.d.

Roper, M., 'Advanced technical media: the conservation and storage of audiovisual and machine-readable records', *JSA*, 7, pp. 106–112, 1982.

Roper, M., 'Data processing', *Records Management*, 8, Society of Archivists, pp. 25–28, 1983.

Roper, M., 'New information technology and archives', *UJISLAA*, 4, pp. 107–113, 1982.

Smithsonian Institution Collections Information System, *A plan for the acquisition of an integrated generalised collections management information system*, Washington DC, April 1984.

Sung, C.H., *Archives and manuscripts: reprography*, SAA Basic Manuals, 1982.

Teague, S.J., 'Archival records, Henry VIII to Salt Lake City in microform', *International Journal of Micrographics and Video Technology*, 1, pp. 209–211, 1982.

Tsichritzis, D.C. and Lochovsky, F.H., *Data base management systems*, Academic Press, 1977.

Weill, G., *The admissibility of microforms as evidence: a RAMP study*, UNESCO, 1981.

Professional training and research

Cook, M., *Caribbean region: training in archives and records management*, UNESCO, 1983.

Cook, M., *The education and training of archivists: status report of archival training programmes and assessment of manpower needs*, Meeting of experts on the harmonization of archival training programmes, November 1979, UNESCO, 1979.

Cook, M., *Guidelines for curriculum development in records management and the administration of modern archives: a RAMP study*, UNESCO, 1982.

Cook, M., *The teaching of technology as a subject for the preparation of librarians, documentalists, archivists and other information specialists*, International symposium on harmonization of education and training programmes in information science, librarianship and archival studies, Paris, 1984, UNESCO, 1984.

Cox, R.J., 'Bibliography and reference for the archivist', *AA*, 46, pp. 185–187, 1983.

Havard-Williams, P., 'Education and training for archives', *International Library Review*, 14, 2, pp. 199–204, 1982.

Houser, L.J., 'The PhD dissertation in library science', *Library Research*, 4, pp. 95–107, 1982.

Kathpalia, Y.P., *A model curriculum for the training of specialists in documentary preservation and restoration: a RAMP study with guidelines*, UNESCO, 1984.

L'Huillier, H., 'La formation permanente des archivistes français', *Gazette des Archives*, 117/8, pp. 90–102, 1982.

Martyn, J. and Lancaster, F.W., *Investigative methods in library and information science: an introduction*, Information Sources Press, Arlington, Va., 1981.

Neelameghan, A., *Guidelines for formulating policy on the education, training and development of library and information personnel*, UNESCO, 1978.

Rastas, P., *The training of records personnel*, Proceedings of X International Congress on Archives, Bonn, 1984.

Roper, M., 'ADP training for archivists in the British Isles', *ADPA*, 4, pp. 13–16, 1984.

Ruus, L.C.M., 'The training of data services professionals, past, present and future', *Library Trends*, 30, pp. 455–465, 1982.

Wasserman, P., *The teaching of management as a subject for the preparation of librarians, documentalists, archivists and other information specialists*, International symposium on harmonization of education and training programmes in information science, librarianship and archival studies, Paris, 1984, UNESCO, 1984.

Records management

Ben, G.F., Reitzfeld, M. and Roper, W.L., 'A records management glossary', *Records Management*, 2, pp. 2–32, 1964.

Benedon, W., 'The benefits and techniques of modern records management', *Records Management*, Conference at the Shell Centre, London, Society of Archivists, pp. 1–22, 1979.

Benedon, W., *Records Managment*, California, 1969.

Bloomfield, P., 'Plan, control and review: framing a retention policy', *Records Management*, 8, Society of Archivists, pp. 18–24, 1983.

Charman, D., 'Archives and records management: an interface', *JSA*, 6, pp. 423–427, 1980.

Charman, D., 'Records management and the selection of business archives in the UK', *Bulletin of the Committee on Business Archives*, International Council on Archives, 4, pp. 9–11, 1981.

Charman, D., 'Standards and cost-benefit analysis for storage of records in records centres', *Records Management*, 8, Society of Archivists, pp. 10–17, 1983.

Charman, D., *Records surveys and schedules: a RAMP study with guidelines*, UNESCO, 1984.

Cook, M., *Archives administration*, Dawson, 1977, Chs. 3–5.

Diamond, G.Z., *Records management: a practical guide*, AMACOM, 1983.

Duboscq, G., 'Le depot de prearchivage: idée et instrument', *Archivum*, 26, pp. 37–44, 1979.

Dyfed County Council Archives, *Records management procedure*, Carmarthen, 1982.

Hampson, J., *The removal of a records centre and its contents: a case study*, Society of Archivists, 1982.

Hill, D.L., 'Archive material: its selection and preservation', *Records Management*, 7, Society of Archivists, pp. 23–26, 1984.

Hull, F., 'The appraisal of documents: problems and pitfalls', *JSA*, 6, pp. 287–291, 1980.

Hull, F., 'The transfer and documentation of records', *Records Management*, 3, Society of Archivists, pp. 33–43, 1979.

Hull, F., *The use of sampling techniques in the retention of archives: a RAMP study with guidelines*, UNESCO, 1981.

Jackson, B., 'A records management programme', *Records Management*, 5, Society of Archivists, pp. 8–32, 1981.

Knightbridge, A.A., 'Particular instance papers', Sampling PIPs, *RAD Occasional paper no. 8: Proceedings of a seminar, Jan. 1984*, PRO, 1984.

Kromnov, A., 'The appraisal of contemporary records', *Archivum*, 26, pp. 45–55, 1979.

L'Huillier, H., 'La rédaction des bordereaux de versement', *Gazette des Archives*, 115, pp. 203–215, 1981.

Lamb, N., 'Filing systems: indexing and classification', *Records Management*, 1, Society of Archivists, pp. 16–24, 1977.

Newton, S.C. (ed), *Office automation and records management*, Society of Archivists, Records Management Group, 1981.

Newton, S.C., 'Selection and disposal: legal requirements', *Records Management*, 1, Society of Archivists, pp. 43–51, 1977.

Paterson, A. and Cole, M., 'The future of paperwork and information retrieval', *Records Management*, Conference at the Shell Centre, London, Society of Archivists, pp. 41–54, 1979.

PRO, Records Administration Division, *Manual of records administration*, 1983.

Rhoads, J.B., *The role of archives and records management in national information systems*, PGI and UNISIST, UNESCO, 1983.

Ricks, A., 'Records management as an archival function', *Archivum*, 26, pp. 29–36, 1979.

Smith, A.D., *Filing, retrieval and control systems*, Business Equipment Trade Association, London, 1979.

User studies

Archives and the problem of large-scale publications, Actes de la 22e. conference internationale de la table ronde des archives, Pressburg, 1984.

Berche, C., 'L'utilisation des archives par le grand public', *Archivum*, 29, pp. 113–123, 1982.

Borsa, I., 'The expanding archival clientèle in the post-world war II period', *Archivum*, 26, pp. 127–136, 1979.

Casterline, G.F., *Archives and manuscripts: exhibits*, SAA Basic Manuals, 1980.

Duchein, M., *Obstacles to access, use and transfer of information from archives: a RAMP study*, UNESCO, 1983.

Freeman, E.T., 'In the eye of the beholder: archive administration from the user's point of view', *AA*, 47, pp. 111–123, 1984.

Garcia Belsunce, C.A., 'El uso practico de los archivos', *Archivum*, 29, pp. 77–86, 1982.

Hildesheimer, F., 'Inventaires d'archives et recherche historique', *Gazette des Archives*, 117/8, pp. 71–80, 1982.

L'information et l'orientation des utilisateurs des archives, Actes de la 20e. conference internationale de la table ronde des archives, Oslo, 1982.

Joyce, W.L., 'Archivists and research use', *AA*, 47, pp. 124–133, 1984.

Pardo, T.C., *Basic archival workshops: a handbook for the workshop organiser*, SAA, 1982.

Pederson, A.E. and Farr, G., *Archives and manuscripts: public programs*, SAA Basic Manuals, 1982.

Peterson, T.H., 'After five years: an assessment of the amended freedom of information act', *AA*, 43, pp. 161–168, 1980.

Prasad, S.N., 'The liberalisation of access and use', *Archivum*, 26, pp. 137–144, 1979.

Principe, L.R., 'Everyman and archives', *Archivum*, 29, pp. 135–142, 1982.

Rhoads, J.B., *The applicability of UNISIST guidelines and ISO international standards to archives administration and records management: a RAMP study*, UNESCO, 1982.

Roper, M., 'Academic use of archives', *Archivum*, 29, pp. 27—45, 1982.

Sene, H., *The teaching of user studies as a subject for the preparation of librarians, documentalists, archivists and other information specialists*, International symposium of harmonization of education and training programmes in information science, librarianship and archival studies, October 1984, PGI and UNISIST, UNESCO, 1984.

Speakman, M.S., 'The user talks back', *AA*, 47, pp. 164—171, 1984.

Symposium of editors of documentation, library and archives journals, *Bibliography, Documentation, Terminology*, 12 (July 1972).

Taylor, H.A., *Archival services and the concept of the user: a RAMP study*, UNESCO, 1984.

UNISIST, *Guidelines on studies of information users* (pilot version), UNESCO, 1981.

Index

AACR2 6, 121–2, 127, 146

abstract 60, 80, 108–9, 114; as data element 130–1, 141

access: to archival materials 21, 24, 68, 103; category, as data element 135–6; control, automated 177; costs 77; facilities 15, 34, 182–3; to finding aids 123–4; legal control of 36; multi-site 168, 175; policy 18–19, 135–6; public right of 19, 62, 184–5; record, as data element 133; remote 176; restrictions 132–3, 183–4; in records managment 19, 55, 58, 60, 62, 183–5

accession number 94, 100; record, as data element 134; register 78, 113, 134

accessioning 31–2, 78

accounting records 95

accrual of records 55, 89, 117, 134–5

acknowledgement of transfer 78

acquisition of archival materials 5–9, 19–21, 65–6, 181; policy 31–2, 185; as data element 134

added entry 104

administrative control 33, 55–6, 78, 81, 86–7, 103, 105, 113, 134–7, 154; arrangement in 79, 88; automated 161; informa-

tion, as data element 134–5; instruments 91–2; in records management 58–9, 63; representations for 106

administrative history 71, 81, 105, 123; class level 115; group level 113; as data element 128–9, 141; in searches 140–1; value of 52–3, 65, 68, 70, 72, 77

alphabetical arrangement 97–8; code 91–2, 94, 100

alphabeticisation 146–7

analysis of materials 80–1

appraisal 5–6, 9, 23, 51–2, 70, 73, 76–7, 135, 181, 188; in archives management 52, 65, 68–72; cost in 51, 62, 73–4; defined 65; in records management 32, 43, 50–3, 56; retrospective 52, 76–7

appraisal, theory of 72–5

ARCAIC 172

archival description project 4, 122, 125; sector 127–34

archival development model 28ff

archival order 33, 79, 91–2 see also original order, provenance

archival relationships 86 see also arrangement of archival materials

archival value 77 see also appraisal

219

filing system 42, 63, 88—9, 115

film archives 8, 24, 183

finding aid 67, 101, 103, 135—6, 170, 179, 185; access to 123—4; bias in 115, 118—19; computer-produced 120, 154; design of 105, 111—12, 189; indexes in 139—42; multi-repository 82, 91—2, 108, 119—21; published 28, 106—8, 133; in records management 58, 60, 74; standard for 185; subject-based 123 *see also* representation; system 10, 34, 43, 79, 106—8, 120; user response to 122—4

flowchart 44

forms management 42—3

FORTRAN 174

freedom of information 18 —19, 26, 184—6

freelance service 27

free text: abstract 141; field 108—9, 130—2, 168—9; description, keywords in 113—14; package 171; searching 161

frequency of reference 62, 77, 89, 135, 160, 178

fumigation 135

function: arrangement by 97—8; defines subgroup 87

funds: as data element 134 —5

genealogy 72, 186

Glasgow 76, 172—4

GOS 172—4

Greater London 22, 155

Grigg Report 1, 52—3, 68—70, 72

group 81—2; defined 86—7 description 105, 113, 128; set of 106—8, 169—70; reference code 99

guide 85, 106—9, 168, 170; defined 168—9; multi-repository 108, 119—20

Hampshire 108, 119—20

handlist 168—70

hard copy 176—7

hard disk 175

hardware 165, 174—6

harmonisation of training 29—30

Hatfield 26

headnote 105, 108, 111, 114, 141, 168—70; defined 109

health archives 18 *see also* hospital archives, medical archives

health and safety 39

Hensen, S.L. 122

Heriott-Watt 25

heritage 15—17

higher-level description *see* macro level description

Historical Manuscripts Commission 27—8, 110, 120

historical manuscripts tradition 5—6, 189

historical studies 182, 188—9

hit (in search) 158

Holmes, O.W. 83

horizontal description set 106—9, 168—70

hospital archives 92, 161 *see also* health archives, medical archives

hours: opening 184 *see also* searchroom

prediction of research trend 75—6
Presidential Library 26
primary value 70
print-wheel 176
printer 176—7
printing *see* reprographics
printout 154, 176—7
prints 189
priorities: in archives service 100, 111—12, 184
private papers 15, 21, 26—7, 66, 86, 94, 97, 129, 181; arrangement of 87, 97—8; sector, archives in 25—6
probate archives 92
process: archives of 42; control in archives service 78, 105, 134—7, 177
processes in archives service 29—30, 32—3, 79, 133
professional status 29
profile match 60, 157—8, 187
PROFS 173
programming 156—7, 168, 174
prompt: for input 165, 168; in search 131, 156—7
PROMPT 177
PROSPEC(SA) 120, 150, 160—1, 163—4, 171—4, 178
provenance 7, 78, 80—1, 97, 104, 111—12, 141, 189; as data element 129; in group 85—6, 128; in item 89—90
provincial archives 23, 185
public archives tradition 22, 131, 181, 189
Public Record Office 1, 14, 17—18, 66, 68—9, 72—3, 77, 83, 85—6, 90—1, 100, 110, 154, 159—61, 169,

171—2, 177—8, 181—3; guide 106; handbook 108; of Northern Ireland 14—15, 18
public records 15—19, 21, 23, 68, 86, 92
public relations 25
publication of archives 15, 31, 34, 133—4, 182, 188; automated 170; history as data element 133; of finding aids 171, 176, 178
Pugh, R.B. 113
punched card 173
purposive sampling 74—5

Quarter Sessions 90—2

RAMP 74
random access storage 59, 75, 101
Reading 24—5
reappraisal 52, 76—7
record: defined 5—6, 41; group (US) 83, 85, 94—5
records: analyst 3;
centre 3, 32, 50, 53—9, 63; access in 55, 58, 60, 62, 182—5; conservation in 59; inflow into 56—9, 101; inhouse 53—4; offsite 54
manager 38—9, 53—5;
management 1, 3—4, 14, 17, 21—3, 25—7, 29, 35ff, 65, 68—9, 101, 115, 118—19;
access in 19, 55, 58, 60, 62, 183—5; accrual in 117; aims of 31—2, 36, 65—6; appraisal in 68; in archives management 25—6, 65, 189; automation in 159—60, 171, 174—5,

records: analyst (cont.)
management (cont.)
automation in (cont.)
178; costs in 54–6; data elements for 135–6; in information services 43; indexes in 152; in outlying departments 55; processes in 30; structures of 41–3; user services in 182–3, 187

Records Management Group 25–6

Records Management Society 36

records system 42

reference code 96, 98–100, 103, 169, 177; in arrangement 81, 113; at class level 117; field for 108–9, 163; group 91; headnote 109; item 89–90; indicates level 91–5; location 101 *see also* location code; numerical 96–7; obsolete 130; in Public Record Office 83; repository 85; in representation file 119; rules for 91–5; as title 80, 128, 131

reference record: as data element 133

reference room 182

reference service 22, 56, 73 *see also* access, user

register of classes 43–4, 50 –1, 56, 58

registrar of data bases 184– 5

registry 53, 63

religious orders, archives of 27

repair: of archival materials 33, 100, 177–8 *see also* conservation

repair record: as data element 136

repair register 136

repetition 109, 118

reports 43, 59, 113–14, 178

reports management 42

repository code 99

repository level 85

repository process control in 79, 133

representation: principle of 112; rule for 119; use of 103

representation file 79, 103, 112–13; additional 105– 6; bias in 115, 118–19; main 105–6, 122–3, 140; rules for 104–6, 110–12

reproduction 133

reprographics 29, 185 *see also* publication of archives

research: in archives services 15–16, 20, 111–12, 115, 181, 188; finding aids for 115; groups 190; institutions 20, 24–5, 161; machine-readable archives 184–5; privileged 184; in user studies 186; value 51 –3, 68, 70, 73–7

Research Libraries Group 125

researchers: as users 187

resources: for archives services 10–11, 16–17, 22– 3, 67–8, 110, 186

retail, archives of 25

retention 62, 65; period 32 –3, 62–3, 73–4; schedule 50–1, 60, 63

retirement of records 32, 35, 44, 50, 53–4

retrieval: of archives 99, 103, 127, 140; constraints on 114; as data element 135—6; in records management 56—9; in searchroom 190; speed of 54—5, 160—1; strategies for 155—8 *see also* scanning

retrospective appraisal 52, 76—7

retrospective studies 184

reviewing records 50—3, 60, 68—9, 136, 179

RLIN 122, 160

Roper, M. 1

rotation of terms 147, 151—2

Rothschilds 25

Royal Greenwich Observatory 24

rural archives services 22—3

St. John's College 165, 167

sale of archives 130

sampling 74—5

satellite terminal 176

scanning 118, 123, 140, 150

Schellenberg, T.R. 1, 70, 79—80

school: archives of 92—4, 108, 111; use of archives services by 186—7; training, for archivists 29—30 *see also* education

Science Museum 20

scientific archives 20, 25

Scott, P.J. 83, 88

Scottish Record Office 14, 18, 21

screen format 168

script: as data element 132

seal 132, 171

search: on abstract 131—2; difficulties of 157—8; interactive *see* online access; keywords for 114, 155—8; online 63, 147—9, 154—8, 170—1, 173, 175—7; personal names in 140—1; predicted 177; procedure 139, 156—7; secondary 114—15; strategy 123, 139, 148, 157—8; text 161

searchroom 60, 182—4

secondary value 70—1

sectors: in data elements 133—4

security: copying 55; classification 185; in records management 58, 60; reference codes for 99

selection *see* appraisal

selective dissemination of information 60, 187—8

self-indexing archives 142

semantics 145—6, 152

serial code 99—100

series *see* class

Shannon-Weaver 9

shareholders' archives 71, 95

shelf arrangement 59, 104, 114

SHIC 132, 144

shipping archives 76

Smith, G.J. 39

social service 71—2, 186, 188—9

Society of Archivists 4, 27, 125, 143

software 154, 156, 169—75

sort field 104—5, 165, 173

television archives 8, 24, 183
temporary description 100, 112−13
term: indexing see keyword
terminal 154−60, 165−6, 175, 177
terminology 127−8, 185
territorial acquisition field 21−4, 31, 76 see also local archives service
text: management 152, 170, 173−4; processing 170 see also world processor; retrieval from 156 see also information, retrieval
textual notes: as data element 133
theme, indexing 145−6
thesaurus 59, 120, 132, 141, 152
tithe archives 27−8, 93−4
title: of archive material 99, 108; class 56, 88, 109; as data element 130; deed 115−16, 118, 171; elements in 131; honorific 146; of library materials 80; page 109; related to level 128; rule for 130−1
total archives 188−9
truncation 156−7
training 2, 26, 29; curriculum for 29−30, 65; staff 178−9, 185, 188
transcript 72, 110−11
transfer to archives 32−3, 35, 53, 56, 62, 78, 128−9 see also accessioning, retirement of records
transfer list 56, 59, 63, 118 −19, 163
Tyne and Wear 50
typeface 146−7, 165, 176− 7

UKAEA 23
UNESCO 2
university archives services 24−6
update 36, 176
USA 18−19, 39, 185 see also National Archives
urban archives 21−3
user 7, 11, 112; access by 103, 176 see also access; administrative 187; confidence 119; demands 8−9, 23, 30, 72, 101; education 144, 178, 185−7; expert 156−7; friendly system 157, 168; group 186, 188; guide 105−6; needs 112, 145−9, 176, 181−2; number of 182−3; orientation 34; privileged 133, 183−4; profile 187; reference: as data element 135; remote 110, 114; rights of 184−6; search strategy 103, 118, 155−8;
services 22−3, 34, 133, 183;
in records centre 182−3; studies 30, 122−4, 185−6. 188; terms known to 157 −8

validation 165−6
variable field 169
Vatican 26−7
verification 168
vertical description set 106 −9, 169, 171 see also horizontal description set
Victoria and Albert Museum 20
videotape 8, 183
viewdata 38
visual archives 8, 24, 183